P9-DEV-906

Understanding the Holy Land

Answering Questions about the
ISRAELI-PALESTINIAN
Conflict

Understanding the Holy Land

Answering Questions about the

ISRAELI-PALESTINIAN

Conflict

MITCH FRANK

VIKING

VIKING

Published by Penguin Group

Penguin Young Readers Group, 345 Hudson Street, New York, New York 10014, U.S.A.

Penguin Group (Canada), 10 Alcorn Avenue, Toronto, Ontario, Canada M4V 3B2 (a division of Pearson Penguin Canada Inc.)

Penguin Books Ltd, 80 Strand, London WC2R 0RL, England

Penguin Ireland, 25 St Stephen's Green, Dublin 2, Ireland (a division of Penguin Books Ltd)

Penguin Group (Australia), 250 Camberwell Road, Camberwell, Victoria 3124, Australia
(a division of Pearson Australia Group Pty Ltd)

Penguin Books India Pvt Ltd, 11 Community Centre, Panchsheel Park, New Delhi – 110 017, India

Penguin Group (NZ), Cnr Airborne and Rosedale Roads, Albany, Auckland, New Zealand
(a division of Pearson New Zealand Ltd)

Penguin Books (South Africa) (Pty) Ltd, 24 Sturdee Avenue, Rosebank, Johannesburg 2196, South Africa

Penguin Books Ltd, Registered Offices: 80 Strand, London WC2R 0RL, England

First published in 2005 by Viking, a division of Penguin Young Readers Group

10 9 8 7 6 5 4 3 2 1

Copyright © Mitch Frank, 2005
All rights reserved

LIBRARY OF CONGRESS CATALOGING-IN-PUBLICATION DATA
Frank, Mitch.
Understanding the Holy Land : answering questions about the Israeli-Palestinian Conflict / by Mitch Frank.
p. cm.
Includes bibliographical references (p.) and index.
ISBN 0-670-06032-1 (hardcover)
1. Arab-Israeli conflict—Miscellanea. I. Title.
DS119.7.F723 2005
956.9405—dc22
2004014973

This edition ISBN 0-670-06043-7

Printed in U.S.A. / Set in Century Expanded
Book design by Nancy Brennan

PHOTO CREDITS: © Atta Hussein/AFP/Getty Images, p. 27. © Hossam Abu Alan/AFP/Getty Images, p. 78. © Awad Awad/AFP/Getty Images, p. 22. © Felix Bonfils/Getty Images, p. 19. © Charles Bonnay/Time Life Pictures/Getty Images, p. 58. © Stephen Ferry/Getty Images, p. 86. © Fox Photos/Getty Images, pp. 35, 46. © Mahmud Hams/AFP, p. 81. © Hulton Archive/Getty Images, p. 12. © Dmitri Kessel/Time Life Pictures/Getty Images, p. 9. © Keystone/Getty Images, pp. 62, 68, 71. © Menahem Kahana/AFP/Getty Images, p. 126. © Khalil Mazraawi/AFP/Getty Images, p. 121. © Jonathan Neeman/IDF/Getty Images, p. 110. © John Phillips/Time Life Pictures/Getty Images, p. 50. © Frank Scherschel/Time Life Pictures/Getty Images, p. 51. © Amit Shabi/AFP/Getty Images, p. 103. © David Silverman/Getty Images, p. 129. © Gali Tibbon/AFP/Getty Images, p. 97. © Mark Wilson/Getty Images, p. 116.

Map Credits: © Rick Britton, pp. 5, 56–57.

TO MY PARENTS,

for encouraging me to ask questions and follow the truth wherever it leads, and for supporting my dreams.

Contents

Introduction

IT IS THE war we have been watching from our living rooms for years. For more than a century, Palestinians and Israelis have fought over the same small piece of land in the Middle East while much of the Western world has looked on. I remember staring at the news on TV each night when I was growing up and seeing repeated scenes of anger and despair: Palestinian men—some were really boys— throwing rocks at young Israeli soldiers in riot gear; a soldier firing a rifle at the mob, and a Palestinian dropping in pain; ambulances rushing to the scene of a terrorist attack where wounded Israelis wandered around in confusion or sorrow; hundreds of people carrying a dead body to a funeral, chanting and waving flags.

Confronted with such images, it's easy to want to change the channel. The Holy Land is far away from America, and the problems people confront there seem very distant from events in our lives. And those problems are complicated. The conflict involves two different peoples, three religions, all the countries of the Middle East, the United States, and Europe. Some of the arguments in the conflict involve events that occurred four thousand years ago. After years of watching peace talks go nowhere and the violent attacks grow deadlier, many people believe there is no solution to the conflict. So why should we pay any attention?

Because we cannot afford to ignore it. History has proven repeatedly that conflicts in faraway places can have global consequences. In the early 1990s, the nation of Afghanistan was mired in a hopeless civil war that most of the world ignored. A repressive militia called the Taliban was able to take over the country. The Taliban leaders allowed a terrorist organization named al Qaeda to operate within their borders, training hundreds of militants and crafting an attack that would kill almost three thousand Americans on September 11, 2001.

The world is a small place, and conflicts thousands of miles away can have great consequences for us here at home. As Iranian poet Sadi Shirazi wrote, "All human beings are like the organs of a body—when one is afflicted with pain, the others cannot rest in peace." Many people are paying attention to the Israeli-Palestinian conflict, whether we in the United States do or not. Members of the three religions involved, people in Middle Eastern and European countries—they all care about what happens in the Holy Land. The United States is the most powerful nation in the world. We can't afford not to play a role in finding a peaceful solution to the conflict.

To truly make a difference, however, we need to understand the conflict. Just because we see two groups fighting on TV every night doesn't mean we really know why they're fighting. For decades now, Palestinians and Israelis have both been appealing to the world for help and sympathy, but they've also asked us to take sides. The situation is more complicated than just a question of who started the fight. We need to look at both sides' arguments, why they are fighting over this land, and how they see their enemy. Only then can we try to find a way to stop the fighting.

This is not a book about who's wrong and who's right. (Plenty of books out there claim to explain that.) The Israeli-Palestinian conflict isn't a story about good people and evildoers. It's about human beings who want to live in peace and prosperity on the land that their ancestors lived on. They want their children to grow up in safety with the hope of a better future.

1.
What is the Israeli-Palestinian conflict?

THE ISRAELI-PALESTINIAN conflict is a violent ethnic dispute that has raged for more than a century, costing thousands of lives. Two groups of people—Palestinians and Israelis—believe the land Israel sits on belongs to them. Israelis have controlled all of the land for several decades, and Palestinians have fought them to try and take it. Their fight has led to wars, terrorism, and economic suffering.

The conflict is also a religious dispute. Most Israelis are Jewish, and most Palestinians are Muslim. Members of both groups believe the disputed land is sacred ground that God has commanded them to control. Millions of people around the world believe Israel is their religion's Holy Land. It is the birthplace of Judaism and Christianity, two of the world's major religions, and sacred to Islam, a third major religion. Because of the symbolic value of the Holy Land, members of those three faiths around the world follow the conflict closely. To these people, the Holy Land is where prophets walked and key religious events took place. They believe what happens there now directly impacts their lives.

➜ Why is there a conflict?

THE ISRAELI-PALESTINIAN conflict is really about home. All of us want to be able to live in our own homes in safety, to sleep at night without fear. Try to imagine two families who both want to live in the same house. That's what the Holy Land is like. Jews lived there in ancient times, so Jewish Israelis see it as a home they once owned. Most of the Jewish people were kicked out of the Holy Land long ago, and, as a people, they have never lived comfortably and safely anywhere else. They returned to that home in the twentieth century and created a new nation of Israel roughly in the area where the old one had been. This homeland has given them new hope and pride. But the same land is also home to the Palestinians, whose Arab ancestors migrated there in the seventh century. It was not the Palestinians who kicked the Jews out, they just moved in later, after most of the Jews were gone. From their perspective, one day the Jews showed up and started moving in.

In 1919, the British Empire controlled the Holy Land, and called it Palestine. Most of the people living there were Arabs. Some of these Arabs began to lobby for a country of their own. There were also Jews in Palestine. Some belonged to families who had lived there for centuries, but most were recent immigrants who wanted to reclaim the Holy Land for the Jews. They also began to lobby the British for a country of their own.

In 1947, the United Nations decided to split Palestine into two nations: one for the Jews and another for the Palestinians. The Jews accepted the idea, and a year later they established Israel. The Palestinians rejected it, and along with Arab armies from other nations in the Middle East, fought the Jews. The Jews won, and took control of even more of the land than the U.N. had originally given them. The rest of Palestine was held by two Arab nations—Egypt and Jordan. Another war broke out between Israel and Egypt, Jordan, Syria, and Iraq in 1967; the Israelis won again and took over the rest of what had been Palestine.

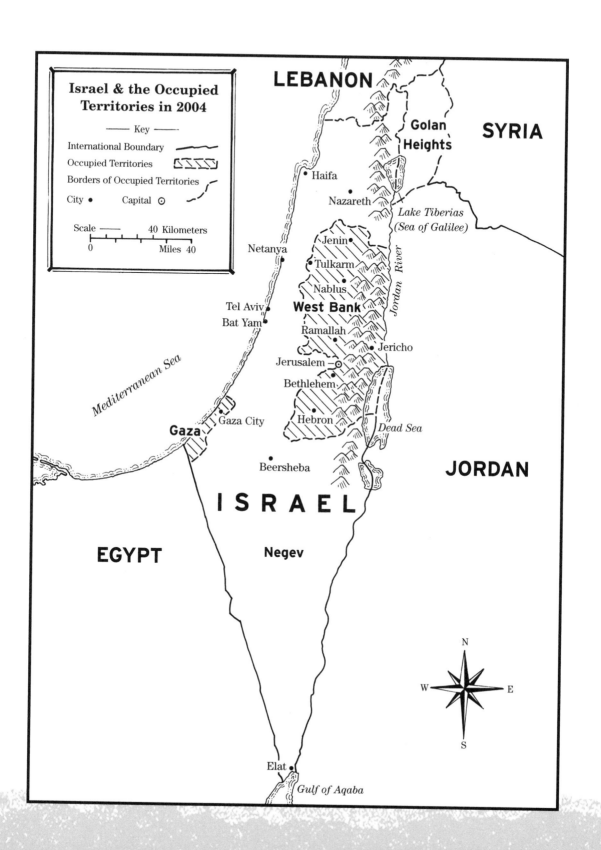

Israel & the Occupied
Territories in 2004

Key

International Boundary
Occupied Territories
Borders of Occupied Territories
City ● Capital ⊙

Scale
0   40 Kilometers
         Miles   40

LEBANON

SYRIA

Golan
Heights

● Haifa

● Nazareth

Lake Tiberias
(Sea of Galilee)

Jenin ●

● Tulkarm

Nablus ●

West Bank

Ramallah ●

● Jericho

Jerusalem ⊙

Bethlehem ●

● Hebron

Dead Sea

Netanya ●

Tel Aviv ●
Bat Yam ●

Mediterranean Sea

Jordan River

● Gaza City
Gaza

Beersheba ●

JORDAN

ISRAEL

EGYPT

Negev

Elat ●

Gulf of Aqaba

N
W   E
S

Today most Palestinians in the Holy Land live in the West Bank and the Gaza Strip, two sections of land, together known as the Occupied Territories, that Israel conquered in 1967. Israel controls the Territories but has not made them officially part of Israel. That means the Palestinians are citizens of no country. Some Palestinians want a nation of their own in the Territories. Others want a nation that would include both the Territories and Israel. On the other side of the conflict, some Israelis believe the Palestinians should have a country in the Territories, while others believe Israel should annex the Territories. So not only do the two sides oppose each other, but they can't agree among themselves on what they want.

Both sides have resorted to violence. Palestinians use deadly terrorist attacks against Israelis. The Israelis counterattack with harsh military force and oppressive rules. The violence hasn't helped either side, and it hasn't made anyone feel more at home. It has led to more fear.

Israelis and Palestinians both have legitimate claims to the land, which increases the bitterness of their dispute. Some Palestinians argue that there is no proof Jews ever lived on the land in ancient times. Some Israelis argue that because there was never an independent nation called Palestine, there are no Palestinians. They are just some Arabs who lived in the area before Israel was founded but who really belong in Syria or Jordan or another Arab country. Neither of these arguments is true, but Israelis and Palestinians are afraid they will weaken their own claims to the land if they acknowledge that the other side also has a legitimate claim.

→ Why is this a religious dispute?

ISRAEL HAS BEEN holy to three faiths for a long time. Approximately four thousand years ago, according to the Jewish Bible, a man named Abraham arrived in the land of Canaan, which is now Israel and the Occupied Territories.

Jews, Christians, and Muslims all believe Abraham was an important figure who founded monotheism, the belief in one God. Before settling in Canaan, Abraham had been known as Abram and had lived in what is now Iraq. Abram was different from most men at that time because he believed in one God; most people believed in multiple gods. According to the Bible, God spoke to Abram frequently. Eventually Abram and his wife, Sarai, made a covenant, or a sacred agreement, with God. They changed their names to Abraham and Sarah and devoted their lives to obeying God's laws. In return, God promised that their family would grow into a nation within a few generations, and God would give that nation the land of Canaan. To Jews, Abraham is the father of their faith and his covenant with God makes Israel sacred.

What are the major religions in Israel?

More than 6 million people live in Israel proper. Roughly 80 percent are Jewish and 20 percent are Muslims or Christians known as Arab Israelis. About 3.5 million people live in the Occupied Territories; of these roughly 84 percent are Muslim, 6 percent are Christian, and 10 percent are Jewish. Most Israelis speak Hebrew, the modernized version of the language of the Jewish Bible, and many also speak English. Most Palestinians speak Arabic, though many also speak Hebrew and English.

Christians also consider Israel the Holy Land because they believe their faith began there. Jesus Christ, who Christians believe is the Messiah and the son of God, lived and died in ancient Israel. Jesus was born, according to the Christian Bible, or New Testament, in Bethlehem, in what is now the West Bank, around 4 B.C.E. At that time, the Roman Empire ruled the area, which it called Palestina. Jesus was teaching in the city of Jerusalem when he was arrested and executed by the Romans. Christians believe he rose from the dead soon afterward. Later, Christians built churches over sites in the Holy Land where they believed important events in Christ's life occurred, and Christian pilgrims from all over the world visit those shrines to this day. Many Christians also believe that when the end of the world comes, Jesus will return to Jerusalem.

Islam was founded in the year 610 C.E. by a prophet named Muhammad in the city of Mecca in what is now Saudi Arabia. Muslims too believe they are descendants of Abraham, and they also believe the Holy Land is sacred. According to Muslim beliefs, Jerusalem is the third holiest city on earth, after Mecca and Medina, an Arabian city Muhammad governed. After Muhammad's death, his Arab followers conquered large territories and built an Islamic empire. They took over Palestina in 638 and called the land Filastin. They changed Jerusalem's name to Al Quds, which means The Holy, and they built a mosque and a shrine on a hill called the Temple Mount, where a Jewish temple had once stood. The land was ruled by Muslims, with one interruption, until the year 1917.

To all three of these faiths, the Holy Land is sacred ground. Jerusalem is especially holy. Shrines to the various faiths dot the landscape. In the town of Hebron, there is a mosque over a cave where both Jews and Muslims believe Abraham is buried. Muslims call this the Mosque of Abraham; Jews call it the Tomb of the Patriarchs. Both pray there. Jews also pray at the Western Wall, a wall on one side of the Temple Mount platform in Jerusalem that they believe is the last standing part of their ancient temple. Muslims pray above them on top of the mount at two holy sites: al-Aqsa Mosque and the Dome of the Rock.

➜ Why is the rest of the world involved?

BECAUSE OF THIS land's importance to three major Western religions, many other nations have gotten involved in the conflict. Many have taken sides. Most of Israel's Arab neighbors won't even recognize it as a legitimate country; they believe the land belongs to the Palestinians. The United States is Israel's strongest ally, a longtime friend, though it has pushed for a peaceful solution for both sides. Countries in Europe, including France, England, and Spain, have tried to negotiate an end to the fighting. There are ethnic conflicts all over the world that kill many people every year, but this conflict in the Holy Land receives more attention than any other.

➜ Where is Israel?

ISRAEL IS IN the heart of the Middle East, part of an ancient area known as the Fertile Crescent, where many of the world's earliest civilizations developed. Its neighbors are Lebanon and Syria to the north, Jordan to the east, and Egypt to the south (see map, p. 5). To its west is the Mediterranean Sea. Israel is a small

The Sea of Galilee in northern Israel seen from the shade of a tree.

9

country, about 7,800 square miles, roughly the size of the state of New Jersey. That does not include the West Bank and the Gaza Strip, the areas known as the Occupied Territories, which are controlled by Israel but not officially a part of the country. Most Palestinians live in the Territories, which are about 2,400 square miles total.

There are four rough geographic areas in Israel and the Occupied Territories. In the north are the fertile hills and valleys of Galilee. Most of the southern half of the country is the empty Negev desert. Running alongside the Mediterranean Sea in the west is the coastal plain, home to large cities like Jaffa, Tel Aviv, and Haifa. To the east is an area of tall, rocky hills once known as Judea and Samaria but now called the West Bank (the name comes from its location on the west bank of the Jordan River). Much of the country is beautiful, with places that are lush and places that are desolate. There are palm trees, olive groves, and sandy cliffs. The capital of Israel, Jerusalem, sits in the center of the country, where the rocky hills meet the coastal plain. It is one of the holiest cities on earth.

Not only is Israel small, but very little of the land is good for farming. The Negev is largely barren, and many other parts of the country are too sandy, swampy, or rocky for crops. In the roughly 20 percent of the land that is suitable for farming, oranges, dates, and other crops are grown. A larger share of the economy is devoted to service and industries like high-tech and chemical manufacturing and diamond processing. In the Occupied Territories, farming is even more limited, and industry is small-scale—mostly textiles and soap manufacturing. Many of the residents travel to Israel daily to work at construction, service, or odd jobs.

2.
Who were the Israelis before there was a state of Israel?

ISRAEL IS A Jewish nation. The official language is Hebrew, the ancient language of the Jewish people. The currency is the shekel, a coin from the Bible. The flag has a star of David, the symbol of Judaism, on it. Israel defines itself by its religion. The Jewish settlers who founded the nation based their claim to the land on the fact that their ancient Jewish ancestors had lived there and that the Jewish Bible had promised them that land. Today about 80 percent of Israelis are Jews. So to understand who the Israelis are, it's crucial to understand Judaism and its link to this land.

➜ How did Judaism begin?

"THE LORD SAID to Abram, 'Go forth from your native land and from your father's house to the land that I will show you. I will make of you a great nation; And I will bless you, I will make your name great.'"

This is the first passage in the Jewish Bible, or Tanach, in which God speaks to Abram (later called Abraham), commanding him to leave everything he has known behind and travel to the land of Canaan, now Israel and the Occupied Territories. Historians and archaeologists do not know if Abraham really existed, but if he did, he would have lived around the year 1900 B.C.E. Jews believe God's command to leave home was the first of ten trials God tested his prophet with. Once Abraham passed all ten, God made a covenant with him that, in return for his faith, God would create a nation for him. "I will give to you and your offspring after you the land of your sojourns—the whole land of Canaan—as an everlasting possession." So Jews believe that from the time of Abraham, the Holy Land belonged to them.

This map shows where the Twelve Tribes of Israel lived according to the Tanach.

Abraham's grandson, Jacob, also known as Israel, had to leave the land, however, when a famine threatened his family with starvation. He and his twelve sons traveled to Egypt, where they found plenty of food. But years later, the Egyptians enslaved Jacob's descendants, fearing that they would help Egypt's enemies. The Tanach says the Jews endured centuries of slavery in Egypt.

Jews believe God renewed his covenant around 1250 B.C.E, when God commanded the Jewish prophet Moses to tell the Egyptians to free the slaves. Moses led the Jews out of Egypt, into the Sinai desert, where God gave them the Ten Commandments and the laws of their faith. Sometime around the year 1200 B.C.E., the Jews entered the land of Canaan, and according to the biblical book of Joshua, they conquered much of the country occupied by various Canaanite peoples and named it Israel. (This ancient Kingdom of Israel should not be confused with the modern nation of Israel.)

Historians and archaeologists have not been able to confirm whether the Exodus from Egypt really happened, but they do believe that a new group of tribes began appearing in what is now the West Bank around 1200 B.C.E. and that these tribes eventually gained control of at least part of Canaan and founded the Kingdom of Israel. The kingdom was most powerful around 1000 B.C.E., during the reigns of King David and his son King Solomon. David conquered even more of Canaan, including the city of Jerusalem. Solomon turned Israel into a prosperous trading nation and built a great temple dedicated to God on top of a mountain in Jerusalem.

➤ How did ancient Israel fall?

HISTORY IS FULL of rising and declining nations, and ancient Israel was no different. According to the Tanach, after Solomon died, around 930 B.C.E., the country split into two weaker nations: Israel in the north and Judah in the south. Larger, more powerful nations forming in other parts of the Middle East threatened to invade Israel and Judah. In 722 B.C.E., nearby Assyria (now northern Iraq) conquered Israel and deported thousands of Israelis to Assyria. Judah became the only Jewish nation. In the next century, Babylon, a country located in what is now southern Iraq, became the most powerful nation in the region. When Judah resisted its control in 586 B.C.E., the Babylonians conquered the country, destroyed Solomon's temple, and deported the most educated and powerful Jews to Babylon. Another group of Judeans fled to Egypt.

How did Judaism evolve during the Roman occupation?

EVEN WHEN THE Jews were ruled by others, their religion had great influence. The ancient Greeks and Romans adopted some Jewish principles. During the period when Jesus was living, a new movement of rabbis, or Jewish teachers, changed Judaism into a more humane, caring religion. Rabbi Hillel, one of the most prominent rabbis, summed up the code of Judaism as "That which is hateful to you, do not do to your neighbor. That is the whole Torah; the rest is commentary." This movement heavily influenced the new religion of Christianity, which began as an offshoot of Judaism. The rabbis began to write down their long tradition of oral law in the third century C.E. They called these collections of laws the Mishna. In the fifth and sixth centuries, rabbis wrote down their discussions on the Mishna and called it the Talmud. Many laws and ethical beliefs in modern-day America and Europe are based on these works.

Even though the Jews no longer had a nation, their religion kept them together. Many of the laws and beliefs of modern Judaism were developed by teachers during the Babylonian exile as a way of giving the Jews a common identity even while they were ruled by foreigners. By keeping these laws, Jews reminded themselves of God every day.

A new empire—Persia—conquered Babylon forty-seven years after the destruction of Solomon's temple, and the Persian king gave the exiled Jews permission to return to their land. Most, however, had grown comfortable in their new country and decided not to go back. Since then, there have always been more Jews living outside of the Holy Land than in the Holy Land itself. Jews not living in the Holy Land are called the Diaspora. Those who did return resettled their land, which remained a Persian province, and, according to the Tanach, constructed a new temple on the ruins of the first one atop the Temple Mount. But the Jewish community continued to be pushed around by stronger countries. In 332

B.C.E., the Greeks conquered the region and changed the name to Judea. Finally, in 45 B.C.E., the Roman Empire, the largest on earth, took over and renamed the region Palestina.

The Romans controlled the Holy Land during the period when Jesus lived and died. The Jews rebelled against the Romans several times, and the Romans destroyed the temple in 70 C.E. after a four-year rebellion by the Jews. Many Jews moved north to Galilee, which was safer, or out of the area completely. After two more rebellions over the next sixty years, the Romans tore down most of Jerusalem in 135, banned Jews from the city and surrounding areas, and built a new city. Over the next thousand years, Jewish communities migrated all over the world, from northern Europe to central Asia.

Despite living in foreign lands, many Jews hoped to return to Israel one day and reestablish their nation. Many modern Jewish beliefs stem from that desire to end the exile and return to the land of ancient Israel. Of the first five books of the Tanach, four deal with the Exodus and time in the desert journeying toward Israel. This means a significant portion of Jewish teachings centers on reaching the promised land. It is the defining story of the Jewish people. Jewish teachings about the end of the world say that one day God will send a messiah, who will establish a new kingdom of peace and prosperity in Jerusalem.

➤ How were Diaspora Jews treated in other lands?

A GREEK PHILOSOPHER in the first century B.C.E. commented that there were Jews everywhere in the Roman Empire, and it was almost true. Jews were already leaving Palestina and creating communities in cities throughout the empire. Rome itself became home to thousands of Jews and several synagogues, the houses where Jews meet to pray and study. Some Jews remained in Palestina, however, even after being banned from Jerusalem by the Romans.

Understanding the Holy Land

Jewish communities in the Holy Land grew and shrank but remained until modern times.

Although they often achieved success and prosperity, Diaspora Jews were always a minority in their adopted homelands. They spoke their own separate languages: Hebrew or new languages derived from a combination of the languages of their new homes and Hebrew, such as Yiddish in Germany and Ladino in Spain. During Roman times, Jews were often treated harshly, especially as Christianity became the popular faith.

As the Roman Empire came to an end and Europe entered the Middle Ages, Christians frequently made life oppressive for Jews. Beginning in the eleventh century, they often forced Jews to live in separate communities called ghettos. Many European communities forced Jews to wear special badges or clothes to identify themselves as Jewish. Christians passed special laws to govern Jews, prohibiting them from working at certain jobs or owning land, and tried to forcibly convert Jews. A common belief grew among Christians that Jews were guilty of killing Jesus and should be punished for doing so.

In European countries, when bad things happened, non-Jews often blamed their misfortunes on some mysterious, devious action by the Jews. One common tale accused Jews of routinely murdering Christian children to use their blood in their Passover feast—that myth persists even today in some parts of the world. In 1287, the king of England expelled all his country's Jews. In 1306, France followed suit. Between 1347 and 1350, the Black Death swept through Europe, killing more than 25 million people. The deaths were caused by disease, but not knowing this, some people accused the Jews of poisoning wells. Jewish communities were attacked, and over two hundred were destroyed.

Between 1420 and 1491, several large communities in Europe expelled their Jews. In 1492, when King Ferdinand and Queen Isabella successfully conquered the last portion of Spain, which had been held by Muslims, they ordered all Jews to convert to Christianity or leave. More than 150,000 Spanish Jews, known as

Sephardim, left Spain. Most went to Muslim lands, where Jews were usually treated better than in Christian lands. Muslims had conquered Palestina, along with most of the Middle East and North Africa in the past few centuries, and they had lifted many of the restrictions the Christians had imposed on the Jews. The Muslims gave the Jews more economic freedom, allowing them to prosper. Persecution of Jews was less widespread in Muslim lands, but it did happen. Jews did not have the same rights as Muslim citizens did, and, as in Europe, they were sometimes forced to wear badges identifying them as Jewish. No matter where Jews lived in the Diaspora, they were a minority at the mercy of others.

➔ What is Zionism?

ZIONISM IS THE belief that Jews should have a nation of their own in the land that was once ancient Israel. Named for Zion, a hill in Jerusalem and also a nickname for all of ancient Israel, Zionists believe Jews can be safe from the persecution they routinely face in the Diaspora only if they move to their own country.

The first Zionists were European Jews. Europe began to change in the seventeenth and eighteenth centuries during a period called the Enlightenment. Europeans created new, modern philosophies based on reason and individual rights. This led to the easing of old prejudices in some countries. In 1791, the Jews of France were made full citizens. Jews gained expanded rights in other European nations over the next half century. Several Jewish writers, such as Moses Mendelssohn, began arguing for new ideas about Judaism's customs and meaning. This spurred a Jewish enlightenment. Mendelssohn wrote that Judaism fit well in modern Europe because, like the Enlightenment, it called for humanism, morality, and reason.

Jews began to believe they could integrate more with their neighbors, and they shouldn't wait around for a messiah to save them and bring them back to the Holy Land. They began to speak the languages of their neighbors and study in their countries' schools. This led to increased Jewish integration into European society—Jews even took on leadership positions.

But anti-Semitism, or prejudice against Jews, was not gone. In 1791, Czarina Elizabeth I of Russia decreed that all Russian Jews must live in one region, named the Pale of Settlement, in the western part of the country. In the late 1800s, the Russians forced more migrations of Jews. Over a million Jews were relocated by Pale laws. Russian Christians frequently attacked Russian Jewish communities in massacres called pogroms.

In the early twentieth century, Russian leaders created a fake document called the "Protocols of the Elders of Zion," which they claimed was written by Jewish leaders. The Protocols talked of a Jewish plot to secretly control the world. The Russians used the document to spread fear of Jews and prompt further attacks. (Even today, some people think the Protocols are a real document and continue to accuse Jews of trying to control the world.)

Incidents of anti-Semitism were frequent throughout the rest of Europe as well. For example, in 1894, a French Jew and army captain named Alfred Dreyfus was falsely accused of treason. In what historians call the Dreyfus Affair, the French government convicted Dreyfus and sentenced him to life in prison on forged evidence, largely because he was Jewish. He was not exonerated for twelve years. It frightened Jews throughout Europe.

The first Zionists looked at events like these and decided Jews could never be safe as long as they were a minority in foreign lands. In 1862, Zionist Moses Hess wrote that the only place Jews could be at home was in a country of their own, and the Holy Land was a natural choice.

The most famous Zionist was Theodor Herzl, an Austrian journalist. Inspired by the Dreyfus Affair, Herzl wrote a pamphlet called "The Jewish State" in 1896 arguing for a Jewish homeland in the Holy Land, secured by international agreement. Zionism suddenly became popular, as Jews all over Europe debated it. In 1897, Herzl convened a Zionist congress in Switzerland to formally debate ways of establishing a Jewish state. The congress established the Zionist Organization, a group dedicated to creating such a state, and elected Herzl as its first president. The congress met yearly. Herzl himself began lobbying the Sultan, the ruler of the Ottoman Empire, which controlled the Holy Land, to give the Jews a homeland there.

The Sultan rejected the idea, but many Jews were already immigrating to the Holy Land whether he wanted them to or not. Even before Zionism, some Jewish communities remained in what had once been ancient Israel. In 1882, a group of Russian Jews had founded the first Zionist colony on some open land in Galilee, fleeing the violence back in Russia. Many Jews were leaving Russia, though most were immigrating to America. (The United States is home to more Jews today than any other country, including Israel.) But a Russian Jewish organization called Hovevei Zion (Lovers of Zion) had begun helping Jews settle in the Holy Land, sometimes smuggling them past Ottoman authorities, and giving them money. When the Zionist Organization began

Three elderly Jewish settlers in Jerusalem, January 1870.

19

its operations, Hovevei Zion began working with it. The Zionist Organization had two main activities: it lobbied other countries to support the creation of a Jewish state, and it helped Jewish settlers move to the Holy Land. By 1900, Zionists had created twenty-one settlements with 4,500 Jewish residents. Sometimes they settled on open land and sometimes they bought land from local Arab residents. In 1909, they began building a Jewish suburb outside the coastal city of Jaffa. They named it Tel Aviv, and it grew into a city during the next ten years.

Life was not easy for the Jewish settlers. The Ottoman province they were moving to was poor, and living conditions were difficult. Many of the Arabs were uneasy about these strange new settlers. The Zionists had a strong spiritual belief that motivated them to stay, however. Jews call the large waves of migration *aliyas*. The term comes from a word used during worship—it refers to when someone goes to the front of the synagogue to read from the Torah. Zionist Jews saw their return to Palestine as an *aliya*, or a spiritual journey closer to holiness. Even though the later waves of Zionists were not devoutly religious—in fact, many of them were Socialists who did not believe in religion but saw Judaism as an ethnic identity—they still felt a strong connection to the land. All of them, religious or not, had been raised on biblical stories of Galilee, Hebron, and Jerusalem. To walk those lands gave the settlers an intense feeling of belonging. Some secular Zionists were so moved when they first saw the Western Wall of the Temple Mount that they broke down sobbing. They believed being in the Holy Land was all the spirituality they needed. But these Jews were not moving to an empty, deserted land (no more so than the first colonists who settled in America came to an empty land). The Arabs who lived there also claimed the Holy Land as their own.

3.
Who were the Palestinians before they became known as Palestinians?

IT'S EASY TO define who an American is: someone who is born in the United States of America or someone who moves there and becomes a citizen. It's not as easy to define who Palestinians are. There has never been an independent nation called Palestine.

Many Palestinians argue that there has been a Palestinian people since biblical times, even though they did not call themselves Palestinians until recently. They argue that they are descended from the Canaanites or the Philistines, two peoples who were living in Canaan when the ancient Israelites conquered the land. Many Israelis, however, point to the fact that Palestinians did not start calling themselves a people until the twentieth century, at the same time that Jews began immigrating in large numbers to the Holy Land. They argue that different Arab tribes have moved in and out of what is now Israel and the Occupied Territories for more than a thousand years. When Zionists began settling in the land, the Arabs living there reacted by suddenly calling themselves Palestinians and demanding their own country.

The real story is more complicated and requires understanding the Palestinians' roots and why their connection to the Holy Land is just as strong as the Israelis'.

➤ How did the Arabs and Islam come to the Holy Land?

THE PALESTINIANS ARE Arabs, and most are Muslim. In the year 610, the Arabs were an unorganized group of tribes living on the Arabian peninsula, hundreds of miles southeast of Palestina, which was still part of the Roman Empire. Some Arabs were bedouins, fierce warriors and herdsmen who roamed Arabia on camels. Others lived in towns, working as traders. The various tribes often fought one another.

Islam and its prophet, Muhammad ibn Abdullah, unified the Arabs. In 610, Muhammad, a merchant in the town of Mecca, started to preach about Allah, or

The Prophet Muhammad's mosque lit for sunset prayer in Medina, Saudi Arabia. Muhammad is buried in the mosque, which is the second most holy site of Islam.

the God. At that time most Arabs believed in multiple gods, but Muhammad said that Allah was the one and only God. The Arab tribes had spent centuries fighting one another, yet with his new faith, fair leadership, and victory in several battles, Muhammad successfully united them as one people.

The two nearby empires at that time, Rome and Persia, were weak after fighting each other for centuries, and the unified Arabs saw an opportunity to expand their land. In 637 C.E., they took Palestina from the Romans. Within 120 years, they conquered all of Persia, the entire Middle East, and large parts of North Africa and Spain.

The Romans had controlled Palestina for almost seven centuries. Most of the population was Christian, and Jerusalem had become Christianity's most holy city, full of churches and sacred shrines. The Temple Mount, by contrast, was empty

What is Islam?

ACCORDING TO THE Muslim holy book, the Qur'an, Muhammad taught that all Arabs should surrender to Allah—*Islam* means "to surrender"—and accept that Allah created the world, controls all life, and sits in judgment of people after they die. Islam shares many basic beliefs with Judaism and Christianity. However, Muslims believe those two faiths have strayed from the true path to God. Muslims believe in five basic pillars of faith: surrender and accept Allah, pray to him five times daily, give to charity in his name, fast during the days of the holy month of Ramadan, and make a pilgrimage to Mecca at least once. All of these pillars have two main goals: they remind Muslims that there is something greater than themselves, and they create unity in the Muslim community, the Umma.

Muslims believe strongly in community because Muhammad was not just a prophet, he was a community leader. Muhammad believed religion was not something to be thought about just at prayer time but something that should govern all parts of Muslims' lives, from their eating to their sleeping. And it should give them a common identity with other Muslims.

and abandoned—when the Arabs arrived in Jerusalem, they were horrified to find that the Christians had been using the platform where the temple once stood as a garbage dump. To Christians, the mount was a Jewish holy site, with no link to their religion.

To the Muslims, who saw their faith as an extension of Judaism as well as Christianity, the mount was sacred. One of the more well-known chapters in the Qur'an says that Muhammad flew one night with an angel to "the most distant mosque." From there he ascended to heaven, where he spoke with all the other prophets and then Allah before returning to earth. The Qur'an never mentions where the mosque was, but a few years after Muhammad's death, Muslim teachers began to argue that it was in Jerusalem, atop the Temple Mount. No actual mosque stood there yet, but Muslims believed the passage meant one day a mosque would. For Muslims, linking their faith to the holy spots of the other religions, like the mount, gave Islam added stature.

After conquering Palestina (Filastin in Arabic), the Arabs renamed Jerusalem Al Quds, Arabic for "City of the Holy." After a few years, they built a mosque, al Masjid al Aqsa, which means "the most distant mosque," at one end of the Temple Mount, which they began to call al Haram al Sharif, or "the Noble Sanctuary." In 688, they built a shrine called the Dome of the Rock over a rock jutting from the mount that they believe is a holy spot.

→ How did the Holy Land change after the Arabs' conquest?

THE HOLY LAND was now holy to three religions, and members of all three faiths had to live together. Not many Arabs moved in at first, but the general population adopted Arabic as the official language, and within a few centuries, much of the population—Muslim and Christian, but not Jewish—considered themselves Arabs. The Muslims generally treated Christians and Jews better than the

Christians had treated Jews when they ruled the land, but non-Muslims were still second-class citizens. They had religious freedom, but not equality.

Members of the three religions did not always get along, particularly in Jerusalem, where large numbers of all three groups lived together in tight quarters. Constant visits by Christian pilgrims from all over the world created one source of tension. These pilgrims treated Jerusalem as their sacred property and called the Muslims barbaric heathens. They held noisy, crowded celebrations and pronounced Jerusalem a "Christian" city. This irritated the Muslims. And when members of one faith tried to build or renovate a holy building, there was often competition to make it larger or more magnificent than the shrines of the other religions. Occasionally, violence broke out.

In the centuries after Muhammad's life, the Islamic empire grew very large. The Arabs conquered many people, including the Persians in Iran, Berbers in North Africa, and Turkmen and Tajiks in central Asia. The empire became very diverse as many of these peoples converted to Islam, migrated around the empire, and settled in new places, much as Americans today often grow up in one part of the country and settle down in another. These various peoples took leading roles in politics and culture.

The empire did not stay together, however. It split into smaller Muslim empires, which fought one another over the Muslim lands. Over the course of several centuries, various empires conquered the Holy Land. In 1073, Turks took control of it. In 1098, an empire based in Egypt, the Fatimids, took over. But from 638 until 1917, it was always Muslims who ruled the Holy Land—with one exception.

➜ What were the Crusades?

AROUND THE YEAR 1000, the number of Christian pilgrims visiting Jerusalem grew. Europeans increasingly resented that their Holy Land was in the hands of Muslims. In 1095, the Turks who ruled the land north of Filastin were in the middle of a war with a Christian empire, Byzantium. The Byzantine emperor appealed to the pope in Rome for help. Pope Urban II had sent aid to the Byzantines before, but now he had a new idea. He called on every knight in western and central Europe to travel to the Middle East and not only stop the Turks, but conquer the Holy Land for Christianity. He told them God commanded it. This was the start of the first Crusade. Soon sixty thousand knights and soldiers went marching east. Another hundred thousand followed. It was not an easy journey. The crusaders marched and fought the Turks for three years before they reached Filastin, and thousands of soldiers died in battle or of starvation or disease.

In 1099, the crusaders surrounded Jerusalem. The Muslims forced most Christian residents to leave the city, fearful they would help the Christian knights. When the crusaders moved into the city, Muslims and Jews fought them together, realizing these Christians hated them both, but they were outnumbered. The crusaders killed anyone they could get their hands on—thirty thousand men, women, and children died. The knights placed a cross atop the Dome of the Rock.

After another year of fighting, the crusaders conquered all of Filastin—which they named the Kingdom of Jerusalem—and more land up the Mediterranean coast in what is now Lebanon, Syria, and southern Turkey. Once the fighting was over, the knights allowed Jews and Muslims back into the kingdom, but not into the city of Jerusalem itself.

The crusaders had a tough time keeping control of this land so far from Europe. Reinforcements could not easily reach them. Muslims outside the kingdom started a war to take back the land, calling their fight a jihad, or holy war. From 1170 to 1187, a Kurdish Muslim general named Yusuf Salah al Din (whom the European knights called Saladin) led a Muslim army and conquered all the land around the city of Jerusalem. In 1187, Jerusalem was retaken. Saladin allowed the crusaders to surrender the city and flee to Filastin's coast. The fighting was not over though. During the next century, more crusaders arrived and fought for Filastin. The Muslims drove out the last crusaders in 1291.

To many Muslims, the conquest of Jerusalem was a catastrophic event. They had lost the third holiest city of Islam. And even though they eventually reconquered Filastin and Jerusalem, the Muslims, particularly the Arabs in Filastin, never forgot the brief Christian conquest. The Holy Land became more precious to them because they had lost it. And they would remain mistrustful of European Christians for centuries to come.

The Crusades changed the attitudes of people in Filastin forever. Relations among the members of the three religions would never be the same. The Muslims could never trust the Christians, convinced they wanted to take control of the land again. Even though the Jews had helped the Muslims defend Jerusalem, the

Muslims in Jerusalem pray outside the Dome of the Rock in the Haram al Sharif compound.

Muslims did not trust them either. They no longer trusted anyone who might want to possess the land.

Members of all three faiths pushed constantly for more power. They believed that controlling the Holy Land was a symbolic measure of how strong a religion was. After all, many people believed that if your god was the true God, he would help you hold his sacred land. The Muslims let Christians and Jews live in Jerusalem, but they took a handful of churches and synagogues and turned them into mosques.

Five hundred years after the last crusaders were driven out, Europeans again showed up in the Middle East, but as merchants and missionaries, not crusaders. Between 1291 and 1800, the Muslim empire kept growing weaker, while European nations grew stronger. The Ottoman Empire, which took control of Filastin in 1516, had tried to restrict Europeans from conducting significant trade with the Middle East, but by 1800 it could not afford to do that. More and more Muslims began to worry that Christian Europe was taking control of the Holy Land again. The Europeans who came to the Middle East brought new ideas with them. One was nationalism, which would change the Middle East and give Arabs in Filastin a new identity.

➔ Why did the Arabs in Filastin begin to think of themselves as a distinct group of people?

THE PALESTINIANS' ARAB ancestors lived in the areas now called Israel and the Occupied Territories for centuries. But for much of that time, they did not think of themselves as a distinct people. That began to change in the nineteenth century. Arabs throughout the Middle East started to think of themselves not as Muslim citizens of the Ottoman Empire, but as Arabs, a distinct ethnic group. Smaller groups of Arabs, like those in Filastin, began to think of themselves as distinct communities within the Arab world.

One reason for this new Arab nationalism was the steady decline of the Ottoman Turkish government's authority. Arabs felt less loyal to the Muslim empire. In 1805, an Arab general named Mohammed Ali rebelled and took over Egypt. In 1831, he conquered Filastin and put his nephew Ibrahim Pasha in charge of the province. Pasha began to modernize Filastin, which was suffering from a poor economy. He created new local councils, which included Christian and Jewish members. Hoping to begin trading with Europe, he allowed more European diplomats in. Farmers from Filastin began selling citrus fruits and grains to European traders and the economy began to improve.

The Muslims in Filastin and the rest of the Middle East had mixed feelings about increased interaction with Europe. On one hand, increased trade brought new economic success to the area, and with it, education and prosperity. On the other hand, many Muslims resented that this wealth was coming from Christians in Europe. Moreover, the Europeans were colonizing several Middle Eastern areas as the Turks lost control. France took over Algeria in 1830. Great Britain took control of much of Yemen in 1839. The Arabs saw this as a new wave of crusades, and it further energized their sense of Arab nationalism.

The Arabs in Filastin grew unhappy with Pasha, partially because they feared the growing influence of Europeans, but mostly because Pasha was forcibly drafting many of them into his army to fight the Ottoman Turks. In May 1834, people began to riot in the Filastin city of Hebron, then in Nablus and in Jerusalem. Within a few weeks, most people in the province were rebelling. This was the first time the Arabs in Filastin had done anything collectively as one people, and some historians mark it as the first time they felt an identity as a separate group, distinct from other Arabs. But Pasha and his uncle's army crushed the revolt in just two months. Six years later, the Ottoman Turks regained control and the people of Filastin were once again just residents of one province in a Muslim empire.

Their new sense of nationalism wasn't gone however, and it grew as Europe took over more Muslim territory. France took over Tunisia in 1881. Great Britain took control of Egypt in 1882 and Sudan in 1899. And other Europeans—Zionists—were arriving in Filastin. By 1850, there were 5,350 Muslims in Jerusalem, 3,650 Christians, and 6,000 Jews—the first time Jews had been the majority in the city since the Romans had destroyed the temple in 70 C.E. By 1910, 70,000 people lived in the city: 12,000 Muslims, 13,000 Christians, and 45,000 Jews. This Jewish influx spread to the countryside, especially in Galilee and the coastal areas—though the Jews remained a small minority outside of Jerusalem. The Filastin Arabs began to worry. The Jews were paying good money to buy land, much of it underused. But the Filastin Arabs feared the Jews were trying to take over. In 1891, Arab leaders in Jerusalem wrote to the Ottoman Sultan in Constantinople asking him to forbid Jewish immigration. He ignored their request. Filastin Arab groups began lobbying people not to sell land to Jews.

In 1908, a group of young, ambitious Ottoman politicians known as the Young Turks took over the empire's government. Seeing their empire weakening and ethnic groups like the Arabs asserting themselves, they tried a new policy to build stronger loyalty to the empire. They called this Turkification, believing that if everyone felt closer to Turkish culture, the empire could stay together. They encouraged people to speak Turkish, the official language of the empire, rather than Arabic, which was the language of the Qur'an and the most commonly spoken language.

Turkification didn't work. Many Arabs responded by voicing their own identities even more. Arab nationalism was growing. In Filastin, faced with European influences, Jewish influences, and Turkish influences, the Arabs began to stress their own culture. They formed secret societies and held heated debates on their identity. Some Filastin Arabs argued that the Arabs should have their own country. Others said the Filastin Arabs should have their own country, separate from the rest of the Arabs. Others said all Muslims should try to stick together in one country, regardless of ethnicity.

➤ How did the Arabs in Filastin become the Palestinians?

WHILE THIS DEBATE raged, the Ottoman Empire crumbled. In 1914, it entered World War I on the side of its allies Germany and Austria, fighting against Great Britain, France, Russia, and America. But the empire was too poor and too weak to fight. Great Britain attacked the Ottoman Turks and used the new Arab nationalism against them, convincing tribes on the Arabian peninsula to rebel. The British and the Arabs moved up through Filastin and Syria. On December 19, 1917, the British took over Jerusalem. At the end of the war in 1919, they controlled most of the Middle East.

In the peace treaty, the Ottoman Turks kept only what is now Turkey. The last Muslim empire was finished. Arab tribes took control of the Arabian peninsula, now Saudi Arabia. The British and the French divided up the rest of the Middle East into "Mandates," so named because the League of Nations, a new international body similar to the United Nations, mandated that the two European powers control those lands until they were "ready" for independence. In reality, this was colonization. The British and the French carved the land up into separate countries—Iraq, Syria, Lebanon, and Jordan—and installed Arab governments. But they didn't do the same for Filastin.

The British name for the province was Palestine, an English translation of Filastin. During the British rule of Palestine, the Arabs there slowly began calling themselves Palestinians. They accepted the name because they now saw themselves as a distinct people—not just Arabs, but Palestinians. They became more unified because they believed the British were trying to steal their land and give it to another people.

During the war, the Zionist Organization had asked the British government to help the Jews establish a homeland if the British conquered Palestine. In 1917,

31

the British government issued the Balfour Declaration (named for Foreign Secretary Lord Arthur Balfour), which stated that the British would create a Jewish homeland in Palestine. It did not explain if the homeland would be in all or some of Palestine. When the League of Nations put the Balfour Declaration into Britain's mandate to govern Palestine, the Palestinians were horrified. Europeans had promised their land to someone else. The Palestinian people were united by a desire to control their own land.

4.
How did the Israeli-Palestinian conflict begin?

THE SEEDS OF the Israeli-Palestinian conflict were planted in 1917, when the British Empire took control of the Holy Land. Three groups of people lived in the new Mandate of Palestine, and they all had conflicting goals. Britain's objectives in Palestine were contradictory. The Balfour Declaration promised a Jewish homeland but also promised not to infringe on the rights of the Palestinians. That was impossible. The British spent the next thirty years trying to please both the Jews and the Palestinians and keep the peace. They failed miserably.

The Zionists were excited about the Balfour Declaration because it gave them a chance to create a Jewish homeland. They wanted to make it very hard for the British to change their minds. At that time, the population in Palestine was 10 percent Jewish. The Zionists worked to increase the number of Jews in Palestine and create as much of the structure of a future Jewish country as possible.

The Palestinians thought the Balfour Declaration was unfair, and they never got over that. They spent the Mandate period trying to convince the British to revoke it. They were so busy crying foul, however, that they did little to try and prepare for a possible Palestinian country.

➜ What were Great Britain's goals in Palestine?

AT THE END of World War I, Great Britain was one of the most powerful nations on earth. In those days, one measure of a nation's power was how many colonies it possessed. The British had controlled many colonies for hundreds of years, including Canada, India, Australia, and Egypt. The colonies gave the British economic markets to trade with and strategic locations for military bases. In return, the British believed, they were helping the people they colonized by bringing them modern technology, education, Christian values, and progressive politics. The British thought they were passing on all that was great about Great Britain to their colonial subjects. By 1917, European nations had begun to lose their hold on several colonies, as local populations became more sophisticated and demanded to rule themselves, but the British still wanted to add to the number of colonies they controlled.

Some British leaders thought the empire shouldn't bother with Palestine. It had little economic value, other than being a good source of oranges. It did have one strategic value: it gave Britain a buffer zone around the Suez Canal, Britain's most important asset in the Middle East. The canal allowed boats to travel from the Mediterranean to India much more quickly than the other possible route, which went all the way around the southern tip of Africa. But Palestine had a more symbolic value as well. Many British leaders believed it was prestigious to control the Holy Land.

The British government had promised the Zionists that it would create a Jewish homeland in Palestine. As early as 1915, the British government's cabinet had been contemplating moving the army in to take control of Palestine and then giving it to the Jews as a homeland. Prime Minister David Lloyd George was sympathetic to the idea, though he didn't approve it until 1917, two months before the British Army marched into Jerusalem. Ironically, Lloyd George and some of his contemporaries, though not hostile to the Jews, believed some of the anti-Semitic lies popular in Europe. They believed what the fake Protocols of the Elders of Zion suggested, that Jews had vast secret influence in the world through money and media. Years later in his memoirs, Lloyd George wrote that a major reason he supported the idea of the Balfour Declaration was that the Jews had great power in Europe

British soldiers running through the old city of Jerusalem, October 1938.

and America and could determine who won World War I. By promising them a homeland in Palestine, some of the British leaders thought they were making a wartime alliance with an influential group of people.

And many of the British also believed there was something spiritually right in the idea of giving the Jews back the Holy Land. As far back as the 1600s, English authors had written about the idea. Christian tradition held that the Jews would return to the Holy Land before Jesus returned to earth for the Last Judgment. Some of the British thought that by giving the Holy Land to the Jews they were carrying out God's plan.

As for Palestine's other residents, the British seemed to care little about what the Palestinians wanted. They believed that the Arabs in Palestine could always go to other Arab lands and that a Jewish homeland was more important than Palestinians' national aspirations. Foreign Secretary Arthur Balfour wrote, "Zionism, be it right or wrong, good or bad, is rooted in age-long traditions, in present needs and future hopes of far profounder import than the desires of 700,000 Arabs who now inhabit that ancient land." In simpler terms, Balfour believed the

Jews' claim to the Holy Land was more important than the Palestinians' claim to the land.

The Balfour Declaration did state that the Palestinians' rights would not be ignored, but it did not explain how that was possible. In the first years of the Mandate, the British goals seemed to be to keep both sides happy and delay the tough decisions until later. The British created a government, first controlled by the army and later by an appointed governor. They began trying to modernize the Mandate. They commissioned multiple studies of how best to carry out Balfour's intentions and eventually leave the Mandate. They listened to both Zionist and Palestinian leaders, and they tried to keep the two sides from fighting. But as each side's desire to control Palestine grew more intense, keeping the peace became harder.

→ What were the Zionists doing while the British were in charge?

EVEN THOUGH THE British had promised the Zionists a Jewish homeland, there wasn't any guarantee they would actually keep their promise. But the Zionists began setting up groups that would function as a pseudo-government in a Jewish country. They believed if they had a country in everything but name, it would be very hard for the British to change their minds. The Zionist Organization established the Jewish Agency to oversee Jewish affairs in Palestine. Its staff encouraged Jewish immigration, helped organize Jewish land purchases, and handled relations with the British Mandate government. Soon after the Mandate government took charge in 1919, a third immigration wave, an *aliya* of Jews began—thirty-five thousand arrived in a few years. In 1924, a fourth *aliya* began and sixty thousand more Jews immigrated to Palestine during the next seven years. The agency bought large pieces of land for the new immigrants and even tried to buy the land around the Western Wall, which was a Palestinian neighborhood called the Mahgrebi Quarter. The Palestinians refused to sell.

The Zionists got along well with the British Mandate government most of the time. The majority of Zionists were European, and they shared many of the same customs and attitudes as the British officials. They did not always see eye to eye, however. The Zionists were trying to create a Jewish state, while the British were trying to keep the peace. The British officials in Palestine tried to stop some of the Zionists' efforts to purchase new land or bring in new Jewish immigrants because they were upsetting the Palestinians. When that happened, the Zionists lobbied the British government back in England to force the Mandate officials to back down. Their lobbying usually worked.

The agency also helped organize a coalition of labor unions called the Histadrut (an acronym for the Hebrew phrase meaning General Federation of Hebrew Workers in the Land of Israel), which organized public works for the Jewish community, such as large construction projects. The Histadrut's first leader was a prominent Jewish Socialist named David Ben-Gurion, a Polish Jew who had moved to Palestine in 1906. The Zionists also organized a volunteer militia, the Haganah. They knew the Palestinians were not happy with Jewish immigration, and they wanted to be ready to defend themselves if there was any violence.

The Jewish Agency also took over Jewish schools and made sure the children were learning Hebrew. Zionists believed it was important that the Jews in Palestine learn and speak Hebrew because it was one way to prove that they were becoming a new people while they built new lives in a new land. Because most of the Zionists descended from Jews who had been living in Europe as a religious minority for years, they felt they had to break from their European way of life and develop a new nationality. And because they all came from different countries, they wanted a Jewish nationalism to link themselves together. One way to do that was to stop speaking other languages like Yiddish and speak Hebrew, which European Jews had revived in the 1880s. Jewish students in Tel Aviv founded the Battalion for the Defense of the Language to urge Jews to use only

Did all the Jews in Palestine believe in Zionism?

NOT ALL OF the Jews in Palestine were Zionists. In Jerusalem, there were many ultra-Orthodox Jews who did not believe the Jews should be working for a homeland. These ultra-Orthodox families had been living in Jerusalem for several generations, and they would have been living in Palestine even if there had been no Balfour Declaration. They believed that only God's Messiah could restore the nation of Israel. The Messiah, according to prophecies in the Tanach, is a descendant of King David who someday will unite the Jewish people, gather them in the Holy Land, reestablish the Kingdom of Israel, rebuild the Temple, and bring peace to the world. The ultra-Orthodox believed it was not for the Jews to reclaim the Holy Land by themselves. There were some exceptions, however. The Mizrachi were a minor Orthodox sect who believed the secular Zionists were unknowingly doing God's work. The Mizrachi believed Jews had a duty to prepare for the coming of the Messiah. If the Zionists reestablished Israel, the Temple Mount would soon be back under Jewish control, and the Messiah would come.

Hebrew. Chapters made up of young men all over the country gave classes to teach new immigrants Hebrew, but they could also be a bit more forceful. Members handed out pamphlets to anyone they heard speaking Yiddish, urged storekeepers to print their signs in Hebrew—threatening boycotts if they didn't—and heckled speeches given in Yiddish.

The agency lobbied the British Mandate government to make Hebrew one of the official languages of the Mandate. If it was an official language, then in the Zionists' minds Palestine would be one step closer to being a Jewish nation. The British finally relented and began printing all notices and signs in English, Arabic, and Hebrew.

Another way the Zionists tried to create a new identity was through kibbutzim. A kibbutz (kibbutzim is plural) is a collective farm, a village where the members own all the property together. They farm and work together and share the profits. The kibbutzim were also a way to organize new Jewish villages in Palestine's countryside, claiming the land for Jews. Kibbutzim were seen by Jews both in Palestine and in the Diaspora as a noble cause, a way for Jews to reconnect with the very soil of the Holy Land. Not many Jews actually lived on kibbutzim—in 1940, kibbutzim Jews were about 5 percent of the total Jewish population—but those who did settled portions of the land that would later be designated for the Jews in the U.N. partition. Most Jews in Palestine lived in the urban areas, often in the coastal plain around Haifa and Tel Aviv. Jews also lived in Jerusalem.

The Zionists firmly believed for several reasons that the land of Palestine belonged to them. God had promised the land to Abraham and his descendants. Palestine had been only part of a large swath of Arab lands, so the Palestinians (Zionists called them Arabs, refusing to recognize them as a distinct group) had plenty of other places to live. Also, the Zionists were settling and modernizing Palestine. In their opinion, the Arabs had made it a backward, largely desolate land. And the League of Nations—representing the international community—had recognized the Zionists' right to a homeland there when it gave the British a Mandate that accepted the Balfour Declaration.

➡ What were the Palestinians doing while the British were in charge?

THE PALESTINIANS AND the British did not get along as well as the Zionists and British did. The Zionists were mostly from Europe, while the Palestinians were Middle Eastern, had a different culture, and didn't always understand the British. The British certainly didn't understand the Palestinians' culture. Many British officials believed the Palestinians were uneducated and ignorant, and some thought they were inherently dishonest. This made it hard for the Palestinians to lobby the British for control of Palestine.

The Palestinians tried negotiating with the British, refusing to accept the Balfour Declaration. They did not understand why the British had promised what the Palestinians saw as their land to another group of people. Their leaders spent years trying to convince the British to alter the Balfour Declaration, but with no success.

When Palestinian frustration built up it sometimes turned violent. In February 1920, Palestinians attacked two Jewish settlements in northern Palestine and killed several settlers because they believed the Jews were stealing Palestinian land. Two months later, Palestinians in Jerusalem rioted during Muslim celebrations of Nebi Musa, a Muslim holiday dedicated to Moses. As the Palestinians marched in the city streets to mark the holiday and display unity, some attacked Jewish neighborhoods, beating, robbing, and even killing Jews. The violence spread to Jaffa. As the British tried to restore order, some Jews, including a top Zionist leader, Ze'ev Jabotinsky, took up guns and fought back. When the violence ended, 5 Jews and 4 Palestinians were dead. Another 216 Jews, 23 Palestinians, and 7 British soldiers were wounded. Some Palestinians made sporadic attacks on Jews for the next nine years. Zionists made reprisal attacks. But the violence was minor and infrequent from 1920 to 1929.

Unlike the Zionists, the Palestinians had few leaders. One was Hajj Amin al Husseini, the mufti, or Islamic religious leader, of Jerusalem. The British had appointed the mufti in 1921. Palestinians soon saw him as both a spiritual and political leader, particularly because of his efforts to keep Muslim holy sites in Jerusalem firmly under Palestinian control. Eventually he helped organize the Arab Higher Committee, a council of various Palestinian leaders opposed to a Jewish homeland. He was strongly anti-Zionist, but at the same time believed working and negotiating with the British was the best method to get what the Palestinians wanted.

In 1928, just before Yom Kippur, the holiest Jewish holiday, al Husseini complained to the British that Jews worshipping at the Western Wall had erected a screen there. The Orthodox believed men and women should be separated by a screen during worship, but the city rules forbade the Jews to install any structures at the wall. The British removed the screen during services. The Jews were furious. In addition, some Arabs used the passage in front of the wall as a street, leading animals down it or smoking there during services.

Jabotinsky responded by leading his followers in a demonstration at the wall in August 1929. He began calling for a Jewish homeland on both sides of the Jordan River, in Palestine and in what is now Jordan. Muslims held their own protests against Jabotinsky's group. Both sides were ready to fight over any minor incident. When some Palestinians killed a Jewish boy in a fight over a soccer ball and the Zionists held a huge funeral march, riots broke out. Soon another 133 Jews and 110 Palestinians were dead.

The British responded to the violence as they did to all violence in Palestine: they appointed a commission to study what happened and make recommendations. The commission predictably reported that the tensions were caused by Jewish immigration and land purchasing and the Palestinians' angry responses. But nothing was done to address either of these issues.

In the first half of the 1930s, the Palestinians became more radical in their efforts. New groups that were willing to use violence against both the Jews and the British formed, such as Istiqal, which called for all Arabs, both inside and outside Palestine, to create their own country. Islamic groups, which believe all Muslim lands should be governed by Islamic law, also developed. These groups pressured the mufti to stop cooperating with the British. In April 1936, Palestinian militants killed two Jews near Nablus. The next day, Jewish militants responded by killing two Palestinians. The Arab Higher Committee urged all Palestinians to strike, or refuse to go to work. Thousands of Palestinians did. Palestinians began attacking British troops. The Mandate government had to bring in thousands of soldiers and impose martial law. The Arab Revolt, as it was called, raged for three years. The Palestinians now all believed there was only one solution to their problems: force the British and the Zionists to leave Palestine.

The Zionists, who had long believed violence was inevitable, had been importing guns into the Mandate. They were ready to fight back. The British authorized the Haganah to counterattack Palestinian militants. The Zionist militia grew to ten thousand members by the end of the revolt. Jabotinsky had formed a political party of radicals and it called for more aggressive action. Members who served in the Haganah broke off and formed a new group, Irgun Zvai Leumi, Hebrew for "the National Military Organization." Irgun began what it called "preventive" strikes against Palestinian militants, attacking them before they hit Jewish targets. Opponents of Irgun argued that it was attacking without cause Palestinians it considered to be dangerous.

After three years of fighting, most attacks and strikes by the Palestinians ended in 1939. The revolt was over; it had failed to achieve what the Palestinians wanted, and it had cost them a lot. The British exiled most of their leaders, including the mufti, in 1937. Because most Palestinians had been on strike so often, they were suffering economically. And they were no closer to getting a state of their own. The one thing revolt had accomplished was to solidify Palestinian opposition to Zionism and Zionist determination to be tough with the Palestinians. To the British, it was becoming clear there was no happy solution for Palestine—they could not please both sides. The revolt convinced the Jews that a peaceful agreement to give them a homeland was impossible. As Ben-Gurion said, "There is a fundamental conflict. We want the same thing; we both want Palestine."

➤ How did World War II and the Holocaust change the situation in Palestine?

IN THE LAST two decades of the British Mandate, events in Europe had a great effect on the people and the government in Palestine. War weakened the British Empire, and many British leaders grew eager to stop controlling Palestine. And

European Jews experienced a catastrophe that led Zionists to believe the need for a Jewish homeland was more crucial and more urgent than ever before.

In 1933, Adolf Hitler was appointed chancellor of Germany. Hitler was the leader of the Nazi Party, which had won substantial power in the legislature in elections that year. Germany was in bad shape. Its loss in World War I had left the country in economic and political ruin, and the harsh peace treaty that ended the war left the people feeling humiliated. The worldwide Great Depression, which began in 1929, had also hurt Germany. The Nazis gained support by preying on Germans' fears. They blamed the country's problems on Communists and Jews. People were so afraid that they were willing to believe it.

Within two years of becoming chancellor, Hitler disbanded the legislature and gave himself absolute power. He built a police state, organizing multiple police groups that rounded up anyone who disagreed with the Nazis. He began building a large military, employing millions of Germans as soldiers or weapon makers. Hitler focused his wrath on the German Jews. The Nazis used constant propaganda—one-sided information given to people to make them believe something— to tell the Germans that Jews were responsible for their troubles; that Jews were a genetically inferior, impure race; that Jews were less than human. The propaganda made it easier for many Germans to treat the Jews badly. The Nazis passed laws that made Jews noncitizens, forbade the marriage of Jews and Germans, outlawed books by Jews, confiscated Jewish property, and banned Jews from holding certain jobs.

In 1938, the Nazis began an organized campaign of anti-Jewish violence, beginning with Kristallnacht, the "night of broken glass." For two nights in November, mobs attacked Jews and their homes and buildings all over Germany. The mobs burned more than one thousand synagogues, killed ninety-six Jews, and smashed windows everywhere. The Nazi police arrested thirty thousand Jews, blamed them for the violence, and sent them to large prisons called concentration camps where they were detained indefinitely.

The Nazis wanted more land for Germany. Hitler's government had used the threat of force to take over Austria and Czechoslovakia in 1938. In September 1939, Germany invaded Poland. Britain and France, worried about the Nazis' growing power, declared war on Germany. The conflict escalated into World War II, which involved Germany, Japan, and Italy fighting Britain, France, Russia, and the United States. It was fought all over the world, and cost 50 million lives. The world had never seen death on such a horrifying scale.

In 1941, Hitler decided he had a "final solution" to deal with the Jews—the systematic slaughter of all European Jews. At first, Nazi soldiers rounded up Jews, shot them, and buried the bodies. When this went too slowly, the Nazis forced the Jews in Nazi-controlled territory—which by then stretched from conquered France all the way to the outskirts of Moscow—into concentration camps. The Nazis marched many of the Jews into chambers that were then sealed and filled with poisonous gas. The Nazis confiscated the Jews' belongings and burned their bodies. An estimated 3.5 million Jews died in the gas chambers. Thousands more died working as slave labor under terrible conditions. Before Germany surrendered in 1945, the Nazis killed at least 6 million Jews and 5 million other people they considered inferior to Germans, such as Gypsies, homosexuals, and the disabled. People called this murder campaign the Holocaust.

The Holocaust had a strong impact on Palestine. While Hitler was in power, many European Jews living in Germany or in conquered countries escaped by emigrating. The American government and most governments in European nations wouldn't allow more than a small number of Jews into their countries, so many Jews went to Palestine. Between 1932 and 1940, 233,000 Jews entered Palestine in what became known as the fifth *aliya*. Zionists saw the anti-Semitism that European Jews were facing and became more convinced than ever that Jews needed a homeland. When the existence of the Nazi death camps leaked out to the world in 1942, the Zionists wanted something to be done. They thought

Germany's opponents—Britain, the Soviet Union, and America—were not moving fast enough to stop the Nazis.

When Britain entered the war in 1939, many Jews in Palestine had asked to be allowed to fight for the British in a special Jewish brigade. The British government had said it would allow a special brigade only if an equal number of Jews and Palestinians volunteered, but the Palestinians were not eager to help the British after revolting against them for three bitter years. The British Army began unofficially training Haganah units to be prepared in case Germany invaded Palestine. In 1944, the British parliament voted to create a Jewish brigade, which fought in Italy against the Nazis. The brigade adopted a white flag with blue stripes and a star of David. That flag would one day be Israel's.

➤ Why did the British leave Palestine?

ONCE WORLD WAR II was over, Britain started to lose control of Palestine. The long and costly conflict had weakened the British Empire. In the next few decades, its leaders gave up many of their colonies. The aftermath of the Holocaust created more problems for the British. After the war, more than 200,000 European Jews who had survived the Nazis' violence lived in camps set up by the Allies who defeated Germany. The Jews had lost their homes and many wanted to emigrate. The Zionists wanted them in Palestine, but Britain did not. The British had fought for three years against the Palestinian revolt. They knew that another influx of Jews would only agitate the Palestinians and might cause another rebellion. They refused to allow more boatloads of European Jews into Palestine.

Their decision infuriated the Zionists. They had usually gotten along with the British, but the Zionists would not accept this refusal. Those Jews had escaped extermination, and the Zionists believed they deserved new homes in

British soldiers search for survivors at the King David Hotel in Jerusalem after a massive explosion.

Palestine. The Zionists lobbied the American government, which appealed to the British to let the Jews into Palestine. The British still refused. The Zionist Organization demanded that Britain establish a Jewish state in Palestine. When months of appeals did not work, Ben-Gurion ordered the Haganah to attack the British, on October 1, 1945. Now the Zionists were in revolt. They blew up the Palestine railway, which had taken the British years to build. Jews rioted in Tel Aviv. In July 1946, Irgun, now led by Menachem Begin, blew up part of the King David Hotel in Jerusalem, where the British Army had its headquarters, killing ninety-one people.

Meanwhile, the Arab nations surrounding Palestine demanded that Britain establish a nation for Palestinians that would include the entire territory by 1948. The British government gave up and asked the new United Nations to step in and decide Palestine's fate. The U.N. had been created after World War II as a way for nations to work out problems and conflicts without violence. Now the new body would have to decide how to solve the problem in Palestine.

5.
How was Israel founded?

THE UNITED NATIONS tried to find a peaceful solution to the dispute in Palestine by giving both the Jews and the Palestinians their own countries, dividing the Mandate in two. Though they weren't pleased with the idea of not getting all of Palestine, the Zionist leaders accepted the plan, happy to have a homeland. The Palestinians and the Arabs in the rest of the Middle East, however, rejected the solution. They had never accepted the idea of giving up any part of the Holy Land, which they considered theirs. Fighting broke out almost immediately.

➜ What solution did the United Nations propose, and what was the reaction?

THE U.N. SENT a commission to Palestine to study the situation, and on August 31, 1947, it recommended that Palestine be split in half. Half of the land would be given to the Jews, and half to the Palestinians. The U.N. would control Jerusalem and Bethlehem, to prevent fighting over these holy cities. It was not a perfect plan. The U.N. was trying to find the best solution to an impossible problem. This plan, called the partition, created two countries that wrapped around each other, based partially on who lived where. Even with the curving borders, the U.N.

found it impossible to create one majority Jewish state and one majority Palestinian state. The proposed Jewish state would contain slightly more Palestinians than Jews. In November, the U.N. General Assembly approved the plan: thirty-three nations voted yes, thirteen said no, ten sat out the vote. All eleven Muslim member nations voted no.

In Palestine, the Zionist leaders decided that a small country was better than no country, and accepted the plan. Only a third of the population in the Palestine Mandate was Jewish; the Jews couldn't control the Mandate if it became one country and the Palestinian population remained. The Zionists also had a diplomatic reason for accepting the partition. They wanted to appear cooperative, to keep the support of the U.N. Most Zionists knew there would be war no matter what once British troops left. The Palestinians had rejected a partition proposal from the British only ten years earlier, during the Arab Revolt, which would have given them about two-thirds of Palestine. They wouldn't accept only half now.

The Palestinians rejected the plan angrily. From their point of view, the rest of the world could not tell them to give up half their land. They did not realize, however, that their absolute rejection of any solution was hurting their cause. Whether the Palestinians had a legitimate point or not, a large population of Jews now lived in Palestine, the world sympathized with the Jews' desire for a homeland, and the Palestinians' only hope of avoiding war was compromise.

The Palestinians failed to recognize this partially because they still had no real leadership. Their last leader, the mufti, had allied himself with Hitler during the war. That discredited him in the eyes of the United Nations, but he remained the Palestinians' main leader, even though he was now living in exile in Egypt. The Palestinians did not trust the U.N. because it was created by America and European nations. The Palestinians refused to negotiate with those Western nations, still seeing them as colonialists. After three decades of hostility between the Jews and the Palestinians, both sides were ready for a full-scale war.

➔ When did the fighting start?

THE U.N. SET May 15, 1948, as the date the partition would take effect, but the fighting began almost immediately after the assembly's vote in November. Jewish and Palestinian militia groups began attacking each other. In the first few weeks, eighty Jews and ninety Palestinians died. The British would remain in control until May 15, but their soldiers refused to intervene in any fights between the Jews and the Palestinians. They would only protect themselves. For months, there wasn't a full war, but the violence increased every day.

In December 1947, Palestinians rioted in a Jewish market in Jerusalem. Irgun responded by attacking the Palestinian suburbs. The Jews had an important advantage over the Palestinians: an organized army. Even though there were 1.3 million Palestinians and only 620,000 Jews in the Mandate, many of those Jews were young men who had recently immigrated. The Jews had one and a half times as many fighting-age men as the Palestinians did. The Jews also had better guns, many bought and sent by Jews in other countries. The Haganah and the Jewish Brigade had received British training. There were also other Jewish militias such as the Irgun.

The Palestinians had fewer soldiers and they were in less formal units, militias of volunteers, some new and some first formed during the Arab Revolt. The British had killed many of the Palestinians' best fighters and crushed much of their militias' organization during the Arab Revolt. The militias' leaders didn't get along, and many of the Palestinian militias fought one another when they weren't fighting the Jews.

The Arab nations around Palestine weren't helping the situation. The Arab League, an alliance of Arab nations, had pledged to work with the Palestinian leaders of the exiled Arab Higher Committee in Cairo, but the league usually ignored them. The Arab nations did not really see the Palestinians as a people either—they saw them as fellow Arabs and believed Palestine was land that rightfully belonged

Arab League soldiers fighting Israelis for Jerusalem, May 1948.

to the Arabs and should be absorbed by neighboring Arab states. (The Zionists pointed to this as further evidence that there was no Palestinian people—there were only Arabs.) The Arab League sent its own militia force, the Arab Liberation Army, into Palestine to fight the Jews. These Arab units squabbled with the Palestinians.

Fighting intensified between the Jewish militias and the Arab groups and the death toll grew. On April 10, 1948, Irgun attacked a Palestinian village, Deir Yassin, killing at least 120 men, women, and children. Palestinians retaliated by attacking a medical convoy of wounded Irgun men. Irgun attacked Palestinian neighborhoods in Jaffa. Many Palestinians, fearing Irgun attacks, began to flee their homes, the first of what became a flood of refugees to other parts of the Mandate or neighboring countries. The Palestinian populations of big cities like Haifa and Jaffa abandoned entire neighborhoods, leaving ghost towns behind. Many of the Palestinians who fled believed they could return once the fighting was over.

➤ When did the war officially begin?

ON MAY 14, 1948, Ben-Gurion and other Zionist leaders gathered in Tel Aviv and declared an independent nation of Israel. The next day, five Arab nations—Egypt, Syria, Iraq, Jordan, and Lebanon—officially declared war on the new country and sent in their armies. What had been a conflict between militia groups turned into a formal war between armies. The large Arab armies took charge, placing Palestinian fighters under their command. These Arab nations were not invading to create a country for the Palestinians, even though that was what they claimed. They were invading because they saw Palestine as Arab land and wanted to control it.

The Jewish forces were more organized. After they officially created a country, they created an army, the Israel Defense Forces (IDF). As the war continued, more Israelis joined the IDF, giving the Israelis a bigger force than the combined Arab armies. After some initial defeats, the Israelis pushed back the Arabs, taking control of parts of the old Mandate that would have been in the U.N.'s proposed Palestinian country. But the battles were furious at times, and the Israelis failed to take over all of the old Mandate. Neither side could win decisively. Exhausted, most of the Arab armies stopped fighting in November 1948. The Egyptians finally agreed to a cease-fire in January 1949. Almost 16,000 Palestinians had died. About 6,000 Jews and 2,500 other Arabs had died.

David Ben-Gurion just days before he and other Zionist leaders declared Israel a new Jewish nation, May 1948.

→ What was the aftermath?

THE PALESTINIANS HAD predicted complete victory over the Jews, but they and their allies failed to take control of the Jewish areas and even lost ground the U.N. plan would have given them. Even worse, their Arab allies took control of the rest of the old Mandate, refusing to let the Palestinians govern themselves.

Jordan controlled the West Bank and half of Jerusalem, including the Noble Sanctuary; Egypt controlled the Gaza Strip. Jordanian and Israeli forces built walls through the middle of Jerusalem, dividing the city in half, with a small no-man's-land in the middle. Jordan's King Abdullah had himself crowned king of Palestine, claiming the West Bank and Jerusalem for himself. The Egyptians briefly set up a Palestinian government in Gaza, but it had no real power.

The Palestinians call the war in 1948–1949 al Nakba, "the catastrophe." Before the war, they had hoped to have their own country for the first time. During the war, hundreds of thousands, some estimates say one million, fled the fighting. About 300,000 Palestinians escaped into the West Bank and about 180,000 into the Gaza Strip. Roughly 100,000 left for Jordan, 100,000 for Lebanon, 80,000 for Syria, and 7,000 for Egypt. Most had thought they would be able to return once the fighting stopped. But when the U.N. asked Israel to let them back in, Israel refused and passed a law denying the Palestinians any right of return. More than 350 Palestinian villages lay abandoned; the Israelis confiscated the property. After fighting a furious war with the Arabs and Palestinians, the Israelis were not going to let hundreds of thousands of Palestinians move back into their small country. Palestinian families fleeing the fighting tried to return and discovered their homes were on the other side of a border, and they were not allowed back. Only about 150,000 Palestinians remained in Israel. Israel made them citizens but forced them to live in restricted areas for years. These Palestinians who remained in Israel are known as either Arab Israelis or Israeli Arabs.

For the Israelis, the war truly was a miracle. They called it their War of Independence. After two thousand years in exile, the Jews had come home. They had defeated five enemy armies and gained control of three-quarters of the Palestine Mandate. But they were surrounded. Hostile Arab Israelis lived in their country, and hostile Arab nations surrounded it. The Israeli-Palestinian conflict was not over.

6.
How did Arab nations react after Israel's founding?

THE PALESTINIANS WERE not much of a threat to Israel immediately after the Israeli War of Independence. They were scattered across the Middle East. But the Arab nations were a threat. Most Arabs saw Israel as Arab land, and they did not accept Israel's right to exist.

For the next thirty years, Arab countries boycotted Israel, fought four wars against the Jewish nation, and allowed Palestinian terrorist groups to attack Israel from their countries. Hostility toward Israel became an official policy for most Arab governments and filled Arabic culture. As these young countries—many had only recently won their own independence—found their place in the modern world, opposition toward Israel became almost a part of their national identity. And because of the Arabs' hostility, the Israelis made fear and defensiveness a part of their national identity. This Israeli-Arab conflict would have a profound effect on the Israeli-Palestinian conflict.

➔ Why did Arabs care about Israel?

THE ARABS BELIEVED the Zionists had stolen land—holy land—that rightfully belonged to them. From their point of view, the Zionists had not been Jews returning to a homeland, but rather Europeans colonizing part of the Middle East. And Britain and the United States had helped them do it by lobbying the United Nations to create a Jewish state in Palestine. Arabs saw the Zionists as being like the crusaders of the Middle Ages.

The Arabs were very sensitive to the idea of Europeans colonizing the Middle East. Great Britain and France had controlled most of the region up until a few years before Israel's founding. The two colonial nations had installed most of the Arab leaders that were in power when Israel won independence, and many of those leaders still had close ties with Britain and France, usually military alliances. Many Arabs were ashamed that their countries, which were once the heart of a great empire, had been colonized by two European nations.

The Arab leaders had a problem. They needed to prove to their people that they were not puppets of the Europeans, but most were using financial and military aid—money and guns—provided by the Europeans to keep themselves in power. So they redirected their people's hostility from themselves to Israel, vowing to destroy the Jewish nation. They made life so oppressive for Jews living in their countries that within a few years, almost all Middle Eastern Jews, many of whom had been living in their communities for generations, emigrated to Israel. Between 1948 and 1952, almost 65,000 Jews left Egypt, 42,000 left Yemen, and more than 145,000 left Iraq. The Arab League voted for a complete economic boycott of Israel. No Arab state could trade with or recognize Israel. The league put any company that did business with Israel on a blacklist and barred it from trading with Arab countries.

Several of the Arab governments also allowed Palestinian refugees to make small raids into Israel from their countries. Armed groups would sneak across the Israeli border and attack a village or military base. Because these Palestinian guerrillas faced a large possibility of being killed by Israeli soldiers, they called themselves fedayeen—*feday* is Arabic for "one who sacrifices himself." Arab leaders sometimes funded the groups and gave them weapons.

The Arabs' anti-Israeli sentiment became an excuse for their governments not to reform their own countries. These were not democratic leaders. Most treated their subjects oppressively, and many of the people lived in miserable economic conditions. Israel became a scapegoat for the Arabs' problems. The governments controlled the media, which told stories of how Israeli treachery was hurting their nations. Most of the people still disliked the regimes ruling them, but they couldn't do anything about that. They were not allowed to protest against their government—doing that could land them in prison—but they were allowed, even encouraged, to protest against Israel. To this day, several Arab leaders stoke hostility toward Israel, and many of the people have a deep hatred toward Israelis. A popular Egyptian song in 2002 was titled "Death to Israel."

How did Israelis respond to Arab leaders' threats of destruction?

THE ISRAELIS' RESPONSE to all of this hostility was to make their country as self-sufficient as possible. They turned barren stretches of the country into fertile farms, growing enough food that the boycott did not matter. They developed a very capable intelligence service to find out what the Arab governments were planning. They also built a strong military and lobbied other governments for help and support. The French government, eager to have a friendly relationship with Israel, provided a large amount of military aid during Israel's early years, and even helped the Israelis start a nuclear program. The Israelis eventually developed nuclear weapons. The U.S. government refused to provide military aid at first. It was worried about upsetting the Arab nations, whom it also wanted as allies. The U.S. was fighting a Cold War with the other world superpower, the Soviet Union. Neither wanted to fight a real war, because it might involve nuclear weapons. Instead, they built alliances with smaller nations. Both wanted allies in the Middle East because of the large oil deposits there. Eventually, however, America did provide military aid to the Israelis because they wanted Israel as an ally. Much of the Israelis' military equipment today was bought from America.

The Middle East & Central Asia

Istanbul

Ankara ⊙   **TURKEY**

ARMENIA   **AZERBAIJAN**

Caspian Sea

SYRIA   **IRAQ**

Tehran ⊙

LEBANON — *Damascus*

Beirut ⊙ ⊙ *Damascus*

ISRAEL   Baghdad ⊙

IRA

Mediterranean Sea

Jerusalem ⊙ ⊙

Amman   **JORDAN**

KUWAIT

Cairo ⊙   Kuwait

Persian Gulf

EGYPT   **SAUDI ARABIA**

BAHRAIN — ⊙

Medina •   Riyadh ◉   Abu L

QATAR

Jiddah •   **UNITED**
ARAB EMIRATES

Mecca •

Red Sea

SUDAN   Sanaa ⊙   **YEMEN**

ERITREA

Aden •

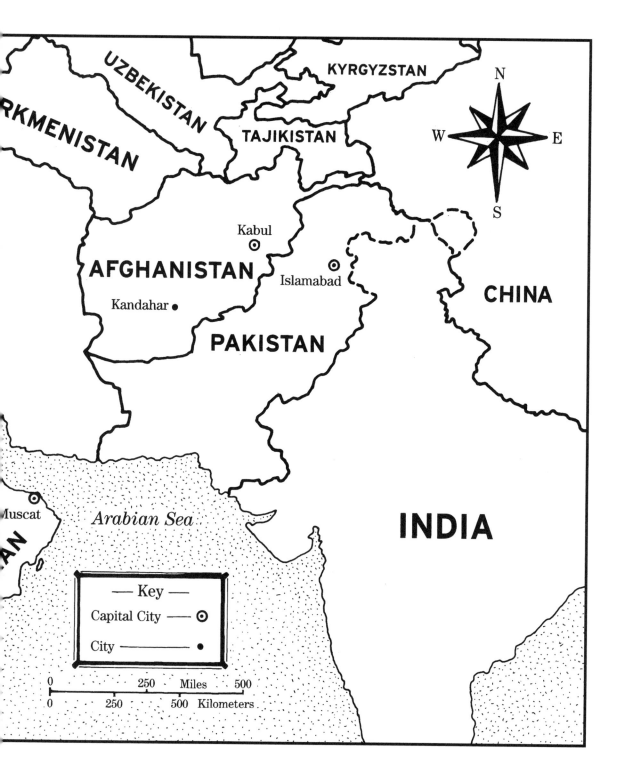

UZBEKISTAN

KYRGYZSTAN

TURKMENISTAN

TAJIKISTAN

N

W   E

S

Kabul
⊙

AFGHANISTAN

Islamabad
⊙

CHINA

Kandahar ●

PAKISTAN

Muscat ⊙

Arabian Sea

INDIA

— Key —

Capital City — ⊙

City — ●

0   250   Miles   500
0   250   500   Kilometers

57

➤ What is pan-Arabism?

PAN-ARABISM IS an ideology that teaches that all Arab states should work together. Many pan-Arabists believe their leading common cause is the fight against outside colonial powers, including Israel. The ideology grew very popular during the 1950s and 1960s as Arabs were still trying to develop their national identities. Pan-Arabism's biggest proponent was Gamal Abdel Nasser, an Egyptian army colonel who deposed his king and took over Egypt in 1952. Once in power, Nasser became very popular with Arabs all over the Middle East, who saw him as Israel's strongest enemy. Pan-Arabism became so popular that Syria and Egypt actually merged governments to become one pan-Arab country from 1958 to 1961.

Gamal Abdel Nasser at the Cairo airport, June 1967.

Pan-Arabism worsened Arab relations with the West and Israel. The U.S. government lobbied Nasser to form an alliance with the United States against the Soviet Union, but Nasser did not want to be seen as a tool of the West and rejected the idea. His independence appealed to many Arabs, even outside Egypt. To increase his popularity, Nasser spoke out against the West and Israel. He broadcast his speeches on radio shows heard in other countries, calling on Arabs to force their governments to be more anti-Western.

Meanwhile, Nasser was allowing

Palestinian fedayeen living in the Gaza Strip and Egypt to raid Israel. Israel usually counterattacked, often sending Unit 101, which was led by a young officer named Ariel Sharon, to attack Palestinians in Gaza and Egypt. Nervous that the attacks would trigger a full-scale war between Egypt and Israel, Nasser began importing weapons from Czechoslovakia, which was controlled by the Soviets. (The Soviets had promised the U.S. and the U.N. they would not arm the Egyptians. Instead they let their Czech allies do it.)

In 1956, the United States, tired of Nasser's anti-Western attitude, canceled plans to build a dam on the Nile River that would have provided irrigation for the Egyptians. The dam would have been an economic boon. In response, Nasser took possession of the Suez Canal, which was still controlled by the British and French. The canal was an important economic asset. Nasser demanded the British-French corporation operating the canal leave the country. The U.N. backed his decision.

At that point, the British, French, and Israeli governments secretly decided to attack Egypt and overthrow Nasser—the Israelis because they saw Nasser as a danger, and the French and British to resecure the canal. On October 29, 1956, the IDF poured tanks and soldiers into the Sinai Peninsula and the Gaza Strip. Israeli forces clobbered the Egyptian Army, pushing it back across the peninsula. Once Israeli troops had advanced to a short distance from the canal, Britain and France ordered both the Israelis and Egyptians to cease fighting and withdraw their troops ten miles from either side of the canal. Realizing that the British and French were using the war as an excuse to send their own troops into the canal zone, and not wanting to get cut off from the rest of Egypt, the Egyptian forces withdrew to the other side, sinking ships in the canal to block British and French boats. The two European powers bombed the Egyptian Air Force, destroying almost all its planes; sent paratroopers into the canal zone; and took control of it, claiming they were protecting it from the fighting.

Nasser and his government officials thought they might have to surrender. It was the American government that stopped the war, saving Nasser's government by putting diplomatic and economic pressure on the three other nations to cease hostilities and withdraw. The U.S. government was afraid that if the conflict continued, the Soviets would intervene and start a world war. The British, French, and Israeli forces began withdrawing from Sinai within a few days, though the Israelis took a long time to complete their pullback. More than 1,600 Egyptians had died and 215 Egyptian planes had been destroyed. The Israelis lost 190 soldiers; Britain and France lost a total of 26.

Despite his military's poor performance in the Suez War, Nasser looked like a hero to the Arabs because he had resisted the three invaders. Many Arabs saw him as the one Arab leader who stood up to the West. He continued pushing pan-Arabism.

➤ What ended pan-Arabism's power?

PAN-ARABISM IS still an ideology today, but it lost its popularity after the Arabs went to war with Israel again in 1967. Even before that, it had begun to lose its luster to Arabs. Despite the lofty message of Arabs working together, all the pan-Arabist leaders usually looked out for themselves. Nasser wanted all Arabs to work together—as long as Egypt was the leader. That's why the Egyptian and Syrian attempt at a united country, the United Arab Republic, fell apart in 1961—the Syrians accused Nasser of simply trying to control their country.

In 1967, Arab-Israeli hostilities grew so hot that war broke out again. Syria and Israel had been having a dispute over land and water on Israel's northeastern border. Israel was cultivating farmland the Syrians believed belonged to them. Syria's government decided to divert water from the Jordan River, which Israel depended on for drinking water. The Israelis responded by firing shots at the Syrian workers. Syria retaliated by shelling Israeli towns. Israel shot down Syrian fighter planes. Soviet leaders told the Syrian government that the Israelis were preparing to invade, and the Syrians responded by appealing to the rest of the Arab nations for help.

Historical records suggest Nasser was not eager for another war. Unlike most of his fellow Arab leaders, he had fought Israel only a decade earlier and knew the Israelis had the most powerful military in the region. But he had made a treaty with the Syrians and couldn't afford to lose his standing as the leader of the Arabs, so he promised to protect Syria. He moved his tanks into the Sinai Peninsula, which had been demilitarized since the end of the Suez War. He closed off an Israeli shipping lane, and spoke of destroying Israel once and for all. On May 16, 1967, his Radio Cairo broadcast said, "The existence of Israel has continued too long. We welcome the battle we have long awaited. We shall destroy Israel." Jordan and Iraq promised to fight too. Many Israelis heard Nasser's radio threats that he would push the Jews into the Mediterranean Sea and were gripped with fear; they filled the synagogues and prayed that God would save them.

With the Arab nations threatening to invade, the Israeli government decided the best defense was to strike first. On the morning of June 5, the Israeli Air Force (IAF) began a sneak attack. Egyptian pilots at air bases woke up to hear their planes exploding on the runway. The IAF destroyed 304 out of 419 Egyptian aircraft. The jets took out 550 of Egypt's tanks as well. Others waves of IAF planes took out 53 out of 112 Syrian planes and Jordan's entire 28-plane air force. Then the IDF sent tanks and soldiers in three directions: toward Egypt, Jordan, and Syria. The Israelis slowly pushed Egyptian forces back across the Sinai Peninsula in fierce fighting; then the Egyptian minister of defense panicked and ordered all units to retreat across the Suez Canal.

When the fighting first began, the Jordanians had shelled Tel Aviv and the Israeli half of Jerusalem. But IDF brigades soon moved into the West Bank and East Jerusalem and forced the Jordanians to flee across the Jordan River. For the first four days of fighting, Israel made no move on its border with Syria. This border was difficult to attack because the Syrian forces were positioned on a hillside called the Golan Heights, allowing them to fire down on Israeli troops. But on June 9, Israeli forces shelled the Heights and began pushing up the hill. The next day, the Syrians fled. In what became known as the Six-Day War, the Israelis took control of the Golan Heights, the West Bank and East Jerusalem, the Gaza Strip, and the Sinai Peninsula. More than 11,000 Egyptians had died, many from thirst while fighting in the Sinai desert. Almost 2,000 Jordanians and 700 Syrians had died, along with close to 4,000 Palestinians in the West Bank and Gaza. Israel had lost 780 men. The Arabs were humiliated—for all their bragging, they couldn't defeat this tiny Jewish nation. Because Nasser led the Arabs in the buildup to war, his prestige suffered and pan-Arabism was largely extinguished.

Israeli forces advancing in tanks in the Sinai Desert during the Six-Day War, June 1967.

Shortly after the war ended, the United Nations passed Resolution 242, which called on Israel to withdraw from territories it had taken control of during the Six-Day War. The U.N. called on the Arab countries in return to recognize Israel's borders and its right to exist in peace. But because of their fear of another invasion, Israeli leaders refused to withdraw from the occupied territories.

Those territories gave Israel a buffer zone in case of a new invasion. The Arab countries refused to recognize Israel. They may have been humiliated, but they weren't going to make peace.

➔ How did Israeli-Arab relations change after the Six-Day War?

FOR THE FIRST six years after the war, most Arab countries made no serious move to destroy Israel, even though their leaders still verbally threatened to. They could not afford another war. Instead, the Arab League encouraged Palestinian groups to increase their attacks against Israel. The Palestinians were happy to take control of what they saw as their struggle, and these militant groups soon became a greater threat to Israel.

Nasser, however, was furious about losing control of the Sinai. In 1969, he began the one-year War of Attrition with Israel. This was not an all-out war, but it was bloody. Egyptian forces shelled Israeli troops stationed in the Sinai Peninsula. The Israelis responded by bombing Egypt. This back-and-forth went on for a year, until the U.S. government negotiated a cease-fire.

In 1970, Nasser died suddenly of a heart attack. His successor, Anwar Sadat, also wanted to get the Sinai Peninsula back from Israel. He tried to negotiate secretly with the Israelis, but he had no luck. So on October 6, 1973, on Yom Kippur, Egypt and Syria again invaded Israel. The Arabs hoped to surprise Israelis by attacking on a holiday when many would be praying.

The plan worked at first. Israeli forces were taken by surprise in both the Golan Heights and Sinai. It took five days before IDF tanks in the Heights began pushing the Syrians back. In Sinai, the Israelis were thrown back ten miles. Fighting bogged down. Then Ariel Sharon led a risky counterattack and broke through the Egyptian lines. His forces crossed over the canal and began pushing toward Cairo, the Egyptian capital. Meanwhile, IDF troops attacking Syria advanced to just twenty-five miles outside the Syrian capital of Damascus and began shelling the city. Both Arab nations asked for a cease-fire, which went into effect on October 25. More than 9,000 Egyptians, 3,500 Syrians, and 2,500 Israelis had died in the fighting. Shortly afterward, Israel's forces withdrew to its 1967 borders.

The Israelis had beaten back the surprise attack, but they had been caught unaware and poorly prepared, and in the first week of fighting, it had looked as if they might lose. Many Israeli soldiers had died. The people were shaken up by how close the nation had come to defeat and questioned why the government had not seen the invasion coming. Prime Minister Golda Meir and Defense Minister Moshe Dayan eventually resigned because many people thought they had failed to be sufficiently vigilant. When Sadat approached the United States and Israel's new Likud government about peace negotiations, the Israelis were more willing to talk than before.

Sadat was unhappy with Egypt's alliance with the Soviets and wanted to ally with the more wealthy United States. And he still wanted the Sinai Peninsula back. So Sadat began a dialogue with the Israelis, with the United States helping as a mediator. In 1977, Sadat took a surprising step. He went to Israel, addressed the Knesset (the Israeli parliament), and recognized the Jewish nation's right to exist. A year later, he and Menachem Begin, the Israeli prime minister, agreed to make peace at Camp David in the United States. In 1979, they signed the Israel-Egypt peace treaty in Washington, D.C. Israel returned the Sinai Peninsula to Egypt, in return for Egypt's pledge to recognize Israel and its borders. To sweeten the deal, the U.S. began giving military aid to Egypt.

For the first time, an Arab state had made with peace with Israel. Israel learned it was possible to negotiate with the Arabs, offering occupied land for promises of peace. But no other Arab nations started negotiations. Furious at Sadat, the Arab League revoked Egypt's membership. In 1981, Islamist militants assassinated Sadat because they believed he had betrayed all Muslims by making peace with Israel. The rest of the Arab nations were not going to make peace while the Israeli-Palestinian conflict was ongoing.

7.
What is the PLO?

DURING THE 1948 war that Israelis call the Israeli War of Independence and Arabs call the Palestine War or the first Arab-Israeli War, Palestinians had three options. Some stayed in the portion of the land the Israelis claimed and became Arab Israelis. Many more fled to or stayed in the West Bank or Gaza Strip, which were then controlled by Jordan and Egypt. About 20 percent of Palestinians fled the country completely, moving mostly to other Middle Eastern countries. Eventually there would be more Palestinians outside of what had been Palestine than there were inside.

➤ Where did the Palestinians go?

HUNDREDS OF THOUSANDS of Palestinians fled to the countries surrounding Israel: Jordan, Lebanon, Egypt, and Syria. Many lived in refugee camps, miserable shantytowns that were supposed to be temporary but some of which still stand fifty years later. Some of the Palestinians had no belongings when they fled their homes, so they couldn't afford to live anywhere but the camps. Sometimes the countries they moved to wouldn't let them become citizens; other times the Palestinians refused to. The belief was that if they merged into another country completely, there would no longer be a Palestinian people, and they would never return home.

Other Palestinians moved out of the camps and formed active, vibrant communities all over the Middle East. A large Palestinian community developed in Kuwait, and by 1990, it consisted of 400,000 people. Many Palestinians moved to Saudi Arabia and Egypt and even to the United States. In these other countries, Palestinians found opportunities for education and advancement. But the urge to have their own country and the pain of losing their land stayed with many. Their situation did not look good. The Palestinian community, its leaders, and its customs were totally divided and dispersed. The leaders of Arab countries often declared they intended to "liberate" Palestine, but it was not a priority. Their efforts shrank after the Six-Day War. Some of the exiled Palestinians began fighting Israel. They believed terrorism was their best tactic.

➔ Why did Palestinian groups start using terrorism?

THE PALESTINIANS WERE no match for Israel. The Jewish state had the best military in the Middle East, vastly outnumbering the Palestinians who were willing to attack it. It also had one of the world's top intelligence agencies, the Mossad. And the Israelis were not going to sit down and negotiate with the Palestinians. They didn't have to. Most of the world wasn't doing anything about the Palestinians' situation either—there are a lot of problems in the world, and some get ignored. The Palestinians considered themselves at war with the Israelis, but they could never win in a fair fight, so they turned to terrorism.

Terrorism is violence used to strike fear into people for political ends. Terrorists cannot win in a straight battle, so they make targeted attacks against leaders or civilians, in an effort to spread fear. This draws attention to their cause and may scare their opponents into giving them what they want. Terrorism has existed for thousands of years and has often been used by weaker groups to attack stronger groups.

In modern times, terrorists often attack innocent people in order to scare a country and force its leaders to negotiate with them. The public has grown more aware of terrorism in the past century, thanks to mass communication and the media. A top goal of any terrorist group is attention for its cause. For instance, in 1976, a terrorist group trying to promote independence for Croatia, which was then part of Yugoslavia, hijacked a plane in New York and refused to free the passengers unless their leaflets were dropped over major U.S. cities. Very different people with very different causes have used terror as a weapon. In the late 1800s and early 1900s, when American corporations refused to allow the formation of labor unions or to give their workers more rights, terrorists bombed some factories. In 1950, a Puerto Rican seeking independence for the U.S. territory tried to assassinate President Harry Truman. On September 11, 2001, in one of the worst terrorist attacks ever, members of al Qaeda, an international Islamist organization, killed close to three thousand people in New York, Washington, D.C., and Pennsylvania in an attempt to start a war between the United States and the Muslim world.

The Palestinians who turned to terrorism used guerrilla tactics at first. Small armed groups of fedayeen would sneak across the Israeli border and attack a village or military base. Many of these attacks were allowed or encouraged by Israel's hostile neighbors, who sometimes funded the groups and gave them weapons. The attacks were a nuisance to Israel, and the military struck back at the fedayeen, but the Palestinians were not a major threat.

➜ How was the PLO founded?

IN 1964, THE Arab League voted to set up an organization to represent the various Palestinian groups. The Palestine Liberation Organization (PLO) held its first meeting in Jerusalem—still controlled by Jordan—that summer. At first, the

PLO had little real impact. Its first chairman, Ahmad Shukari, was approved by the Arab states and was little more than a spokesman for the Palestinians' complaints. Most Arabs believed the Arab nations, not the Palestinians themselves, would defeat Israel and create a Palestinian country. Several of the more radical Palestinian groups in the PLO were frustrated at its lack of real power. One of those groups was Fatah.

Founded in 1958, Fatah, which is an Arabic acronym for the Movement for the Liberation of Palestine, was led by Yasser Arafat, a young Palestinian engineer who had been living in Kuwait. He and two associates started the group, dedicated it to liberating Palestine by violent revolution, and began guerrilla attacks against Israel in 1965, operating from Jordan, Syria, and Lebanon. Fatah's attacks weren't particularly successful, but the movement was good at publicity, which drew attention to the Palestinian cause. In March 1968, Fatah guerrillas engaged the Israelis in a battle near the Jordanian village of Karameh. The battle drew a lot of notice in the Arab world, and Fatah membership swelled to fifteen thousand people.

After the Arabs' defeat in the Six-Day War, Arab leaders were not so anxious to push the Palestinian

Yasser Arafat reads a document in Amman, Jordan, June 1970.

cause anymore; they merely funded the PLO. Members of the PLO removed Shukari from his position as chairman and started moving the organization in a more radical direction—if the Arabs wouldn't fight for Palestinians, the Palestinians would do it themselves. In 1968, members changed the Palestine National Charter to say that armed struggle was the only possible method for liberating Palestine. Based largely on Fatah's popularity after Karameh, the members voted for Arafat to become chairman of the organization in 1969.

Arafat's main strength as leader was his ability to keep factions together. The PLO was an umbrella organization, which means it was made up of many groups with different ideologies who all fit under the umbrella of one common goal—an independent Palestine. The groups included Communists, pan-Arabists, and Islamists. Arafat held them together by trying to keep them all happy. He was also good at dealing with Arab leaders, and went to any country willing to give the Palestinians help. He was very skilled at publicity. He grabbed the world's attention.

To the Palestinians scattered all over the world, this made Arafat not just leader of the PLO but the closest thing to a national leader that they had. At a time when they had no country, Arafat traveled all over the world and met with presidents as if he were a head of state. It elated many Palestinians and infuriated Israelis. To them, Arafat was a terrorist and a criminal.

Because Arafat wanted to represent all Palestinians, including the refugees outside Palestine, he made the PLO's objectives inflexible. There was no talk of trying to get Israel to give the Palestinians a state in the Occupied Territories, because that meant all the Palestinians who had fled their homes in what was now Israel proper could not go back. Arafat demanded a Palestinian country in all of the Palestine Mandate. Israel would have to cease to exist, which the Israelis were never going to allow. It made negotiation impossible.

→ What were the consequences of Palestinian terrorism?

THE PLO GOT most of its attention through terrorism. Some of its members decided that guerrilla strikes on Israel didn't get much publicity and began attacks that would attract international attention. In December 1968, in one of the first large attacks, the Popular Front for the Liberation of Palestine (PFLP), a PLO member, hijacked an Israeli passenger plane in Athens. In 1972, at the Summer Olympics in Munich, eight members of a group called the Black September Organization broke into the building where Israeli athletes were staying, killed two, and took nine hostage. The world watched on TV as German authorities surrounded the building. The terrorists demanded a plane and went to the airport, but a gunfight broke out. Five Palestinians and all nine Israelis were killed. The Mossad eventually hunted down and killed several Palestinians involved in the plot.

The Israelis were not intimidated by the attacks; they responded with fierce counterattacks, and the terrorism made them less willing to negotiate with the Palestinians. They would not be moved by fear. After the Munich hostage episode, Israel bombed Palestinian refugee camps in Jordan and Syria, even though those two countries were not involved in the hostage taking.

While terrorist attacks drew attention to the Palestinian cause, they also made many people think Palestinians were inherently violent or criminal. Palestinians everywhere became associated with terrorism, even if they had nothing to do with the attacks. Any innocent Palestinian ran the danger of extra scrutiny from airport security, or distrust from the person next to them. In fact, many people in the West began to look at all Middle Eastern and Muslim people as wild-eyed terrorists, even though terrorists come from all parts of the world and all religions.

The PLO had a knack for wearing out its welcome, even in Arab countries. By

One of the Black September terrorists who broke into the Munich Olympic Village, killed two members of the Israeli team and took nine others hostage. Eventually all the hostages were killed after a battle at Munich Airport.

1970, Fatah alone had forty thousand members, many of them living in Jordan. Fighters from other PLO groups lived there as well. There were so many armed men, it was like the country had a second army. Eager for their own nation, some of the Palestinian militants began acting like they ran Jordan. PLO fighters would create roadblocks and charge Jordanians tolls to pass through. Some PLO leaders talked of overthrowing Jordan's king and creating a Palestinian government. PFLP leader George Habash, who believed all the current Arab regimes should be overthrown because the rulers were corrupt and dictatorial, antagonized King Hussein constantly. In 1970, PFLP terrorists brought three hijacked airliners to Amman, the Jordanian capital, emptied them of passengers, and blew them up. In response, Hussein formed a military cabinet and ordered his army to disarm all PLO guerrillas. But several PLO leaders declared the northern part of Jordan an independent Palestinian country and attacked the Jordanian Army. The Palestinians actually captured a city at one point. The Jordanian Army attacked Palestinian refugee camps because many of the fighters used them as bases, and refugees were caught in the crossfire. As many as four thousand Palestinians may have died. After the Arab League negotiated a truce, Arafat and much of the PLO relocated to Lebanon.

In 1975, not long after the PLO moved in, civil war began to tear Lebanon apart. Lebanon was a very diverse nation, and various Christian, Sunni Muslim, Shi'ite Muslim, and Druze factions fought to control it. (Druze is a small offshoot of Islam that is now its own religion.) The PLO soon became a new faction. The conflict lasted fifteen years. It was perfect for Arafat's men, because no government was in charge. With his large army of militants and terrorists, he was able to control part of the country. Terrorists snuck over the Israeli border and attacked northern Israel regularly. After Egypt made peace with Israel in 1979, the PLO increased their attacks to prove they were not going to make peace.

Israeli leaders finally decided enough was enough, and in June 1982, the IDF invaded Lebanon. At first, Defense Minister Sharon claimed the Israelis were just creating a twenty-five-mile buffer zone in the southern part of Lebanon to stop terrorists from crossing the border, but the IDF kept moving north, and soon it was outside the capital, Beirut, where Arafat's headquarters was. The PLO was surrounded. The Israelis bombarded the city and demanded that the organization surrender.

To stop the fighting, the U.S. government intervened and negotiated a deal: If the PLO left Lebanon, Israel would stop shelling Beirut and gradually withdraw from Lebanon. The United States would send soldiers to Beirut to help keep peace. On August 21, 1982, Arafat got on a boat and left, moving the entire PLO leadership and most of its fighters to Tunis in North Africa. There, Arafat moved into a five-star hotel.

For all his publicity, money, and militants, Arafat did not have a true professional army. He knew if he had tried to resist Israel in Beirut, the IDF would have crushed the PLO. He chose to leave and live, but his prestige took a major blow. Terrorism was not getting the Palestinians a country. It would be up to the Palestinians left behind, those living in the Occupied Territories, to remind the world of what they wanted.

8.
What is intifada?

WHILE SOME PALESTINIANS in their diaspora were using terrorism to attack Israel, the Palestinians in the West Bank and the Gaza Strip were living under Israeli control. Since 1967, the Occupied Territories and the Palestinians living there have been in a kind of limbo. For political reasons, Israel has not annexed the Territories (though it did annex the eastern half of Jerusalem), so the lands are not officially part of Israel, and the Palestinians aren't citizens of any other country. Two decades after the Six-Day War, they still considered themselves Palestinians and believed they should have their own nation. But as the Territories became more integrated with Israel, the Palestinians lived and worked with the people occupying their land—they started to coexist with the Israelis. It created a conflict of identity. This tension troubled Palestinians until one day they rose up in a revolt against the Israelis, which became known as the intifada.

➔ Why do Israelis want to control the Occupied Territories?

AFTER ALMOST TWENTY years of facing a constant threat of invasion and attacks by fedayeen, the Israelis were grateful, after the Six-Day War, to allow themselves some breathing room by continuing to hold East Jerusalem and the Occupied Territories. There wasn't a realistic prospect for peace with most of their neighbors, so they held on to their buffer zone. But there was a deeper, more heartfelt motivation for holding on to this land, especially the West Bank. That land is called Judea and Samaria by many Israelis, two province names from back in Roman times. Many of the key events in ancient Israel are believed to have taken place there. Abraham lived in this area, near Beersheba and Hebron. The Israelites who settled the land after the Exodus first settled in these areas. Even Israelis who were not religious could not help feeling closer to God when they walked in these lands or visited the ancient towns.

When IDF units first entered the Old City of Jerusalem on June 7, 1967, young soldiers ran to the Western Wall. The IDF's chief rabbi blew the shofar, the ram's horn blown on holy days. General Moshe Dayan, the Israeli defense minister (and a secular Jew), said, "We have returned to our most Holy Places and we shall never leave them." Many Israelis believed their conquest of East Jerusalem and the West Bank was a miracle from God. Within days of taking over East Jerusalem, the Israelis took actions that would make it more difficult for them ever to leave. Jerusalem Mayor Teddy Kollek knocked down the walls that had cut the city in half. On the night of June 10, Kollek gave the 619 Palestinians living in the Mahgrebi neighborhood around the Western Wall three hours to move out of their homes. Bulldozers knocked down the neighborhood to build a large plaza around the Wall so large numbers of Jews could pray there. Israelis began to build large apartment complexes in East Jerusalem to increase the Jewish population in that half of the city. Today, only 13.5 percent of East Jerusalem's population is Palestinian.

Taking over the Territories presented Israelis with a dilemma. The Israelis had founded their nation on two principles: Israel would be a democracy, and it would be Jewish. Because the majority of the population of Israel proper was Jewish (in 1948, Arab Israelis were about 20 percent of the population), the Jews were able to pass laws friendly to the practice of their religion. If Israel decided to permanently annex the Occupied Territories, it would add millions of Palestinians, largely Muslim, to the population. The almost 900,000 Arab Israelis and the 3.2 million Palestinians in the Territories would be almost equal in population to the roughly 4.8 million Jewish Israelis. That largely Muslim population might vote for Israel to no longer be a Jewish state. The other choice if Israel annexed the Territories was to not grant the Palestinians citizenship, which would mean Israel would no longer be a democracy. So Israeli leaders opted for neither choice. They did not relinquish or annex the Territories.

Some Israelis, however, worried that the government might change its mind and give up the Territories in exchange for peace with the Arab nations or the Palestinians. Religious Zionists believed that all of Eretz Yisrael (what Jews believe were the boundaries of ancient Israel) is sacred and must not be given up. They wanted to hold on to the land. On April 4, 1968, Rabbi Moshe Levinger and Rabbi Eliezer Waldman asked the government to let them take a group of Orthodox families into the West Bank to the Park Hotel in Hebron for a week to celebrate the holiday of Passover near Abraham's tomb. They promised that they would stay for only a week, but after the week was over, they vowed to stay forever. The government allowed it, and the families built a settlement named Kiryat Arba.

Kiryat Arba was the first of many religiously motivated settlements built in the West Bank and the Gaza Strip, urged on by Gush Emunim, a religious Zionist organization. Even today, religious settlers continue to construct settlements in the Territories to claim some of the land for Jews and make it harder for the government to leave. If the government ever gives up the Territories, it will have to force these Jewish settlers to move back to Israel. Gush Emunim members believe the Israeli victory in the Six-Day War was a miracle from God, and to give up the lands would be blasphemous.

The Labor Party government that was in power in Israel in 1968 allowed the settlements, refusing to stop them. And the Likud Party, which took power in 1977, actively encouraged them. Many Likud members believed the Occupied Territories should never be given up, and organized the building of more settlements in the West Bank and East Jerusalem. Ariel Sharon was in charge of Likud's settlement program for several years. Land was confiscated from Palestinians to build some of the settlements. By 1987, 50 percent of the land in the West Bank and 30 percent in Gaza had been confiscated, forcing the Palestinians to live in other areas of the Territories.

By 1987, 140,000 Jews lived in parts of Jerusalem that Jordan had controlled only twenty years earlier. Israelis had built 130 settlements in the Territories by then. They built almost 75 percent of those after 1977, when Likud took power. These were not remote outposts like Kiryat Arba, built by religious Israelis. Likud built settlements within driving distance of Jerusalem and Tel Aviv, so young commuters would move there, enticed by special discounts offered by the government. Throughout the eastern part of the West Bank, you can find these settlements today. If you ignore the fact that they are surrounded by heavy security to protect their residents from Palestinian attacks, they look like nice Southern California suburbs. It is easy for the Israelis to imagine these lands are part of their own country. Meanwhile, the Palestinian villages around them look like third-world towns—poor and bleak.

➜ What was life like for the Palestinians in the Occupied Territories?

FROM 1967 TO 1987, the Territories and Israel slowly merged into almost one society. Because the Palestinians were cut off from the other Arab nations, their economy was largely dependent on Israel, which controlled most materials imported or exported. And because the Israelis restricted what kinds of businesses the Palestinians could own, many Palestinians started working for Israelis

Young Palestinian men wait in line to go through an Israeli army checkpoint, May 2004.

as day labor, building houses, clearing tables in restaurants, and landscaping yards. By 1987, 120,000 Palestinians were passing through military checkpoints into Israel every day to go to work at low-paying jobs. Palestinian restaurants served kosher food Orthodox Jews could eat. Some Palestinians even worked on the construction of Israeli settlements in the West Bank or Gaza, sometimes on land confiscated from their own people. Palestinians said it was like working at their own funerals.

Few Palestinians resisted Israeli control. The PLO had some small cells of members in the Territories, and occasionally those cells made small attacks on Israelis, but the Israelis were very quick to break up the cells and arrest the members. Shin Bet, Israel's domestic intelligence service, organized a network of informers among the Palestinians, who would tell them if anyone was plotting an attack. Israel also had special rules in the West Bank that allowed them to arrest someone without explaining why or providing evidence. Sometimes physical abuse was used to pressure arrested Palestinians to confess to crimes.

These were not tactics a democratic government was supposed to use. But for most Israelis, after years of terrorist attacks and threats, such measures seemed necessary. And they worked. In 1987, the IDF needed only 1,200 soldiers to control 1.7 million Palestinians.

Despite the Israeli control, the Palestinians in the Territories began to develop their own nationalism and identity. The generation of Palestinians who had grown up under occupation began to unify against what they saw as their common enemy. Many put the Palestinian flag, banned by the Israelis, on T-shirts or key chains as a quiet form of rebellion. In 1985, Israeli soldiers spent several days shooting down kites the Palestinians were flying, because they had the flag's colors on them.

The Palestinians were torn by their loyalties. On the one hand, if they wanted to hold steady jobs and put food on the table for their children, they had to cooperate with the Israelis. On the other, the occupation felt demeaning. They did not control what they considered their own land. What was worse, they were working for the people who did, aiding and abetting the occupation. The daily lives of the Palestinians were filled with constant reminders of the Israelis' control: the checkpoints, the meager jobs, the fact that Israeli soldiers could come into their houses in the middle of the night and arrest them on the slightest suspicion they were terrorists. All of it made the Palestinians feel like they had no home.

➔ How did the intifada begin?

ON DECEMBER 8, 1987, an Israeli truck driver made a wrong turn in Gaza and plowed into oncoming traffic. Four Palestinian day laborers, residents of the nearby Jabalia refugee camp, were killed in the resulting accident. But there were rumors among the Palestinians that the men had been killed on purpose, as revenge for the stabbing death of a Jewish merchant in Gaza two days earlier. On December 9, some young Palestinians in the refugee camp began pelting Israeli soldiers with rocks. When the young men ran at the troops, one soldier shot and killed a 17-year-old, Hatem Abu Sisi.

When a Palestinian died resisting Israelis during that period, Israeli troops often confiscated the body, burying it late at night with only family members present. The government did this because daytime funerals often led to protests and demonstrations by the Palestinians and further violence. But when troops showed up to confiscate Sisi's body, they were pelted with rocks. The Palestinians in the refugee camp began to riot. The next day, the demonstrations spread to another camp. Within weeks, the entire Occupied Territories were filled with demonstrations and stone-throwing crowds of Palestinians.

The Palestinians called their uprising the intifada, an Arabic word that means "to shake off a slumber." The Palestinians believed their uprising was the awakening of Palestinian nationalism. The Israelis believed it was an organized terrorist campaign.

The Palestinians had resisted the Israelis before, but this was the first protest that spread throughout all of the Territories. Young Palestinians, teenagers and twenty-somethings with no jobs to worry about losing, went out and threw stones at Israeli troops, who fired back with rubber bullets (painful but usually not lethal) and tear gas. Meanwhile, the Palestinians who eventually took control of this rebellion organized strikes by Palestinian businesses and a boycott of Israeli products, in hope of hurting the Israeli economy. They convinced Palestinians working for Israeli security forces to quit their jobs, even though that meant giving up steady paychecks. Pressure from the community forced Shin Bet informers to admit what they had been doing and promise never to help the Israelis again. The intifada made life more difficult for many Palestinians, but it helped them work more closely as a community and develop a stronger unity.

The parts of the intifada that people in the rest of the world saw on television were the gangs of young men throwing rocks. The Palestinians threw stones at heavily armed soldiers and tanks. The Israeli Army did not know how to respond. These men were not bomb- or gun-wielding terrorists and guerrillas; they were kids with rocks. And much of the world was watching. If Israeli tanks opened fire,

A Palestinian boy throws stones at an Israeli bulldozer in Gaza City, February 2004.

Who led the intifada?

THE INTIFADA CREATED a new group of Palestinian leaders, most of whom had grown up in the Territories, not in the diaspora like most PLO leaders. That gave them a different perspective. They were not living in fancy hotels, organizing occasional attacks and holding press conferences to denounce Israel. They were walking off their jobs, running toward tanks armed with rocks. And they knew the Israelis better because they had lived among them. That gave them an advantage. They understood how to hit the Israelis where it hurt. Their strikes caused economic pain for Israelis. Their protests blocked roads, making it difficult for Israelis to travel. Their stone-throwing forced Israelis to watch their soldiers battling kids with rocks on TV each night and listen to the world denounce Israel's behavior. The leaders of the intifada knew how to make Israelis feel angry, confused, and guilty. Most were young and had not been alive during the Israeli War of Independence. Many were more willing to settle for control of just the Occupied Territories than PLO leaders were. They created an organizing committee that coordinated strikes and protests and published propaganda about the revolt.

The intifada also created new types of Palestinian militant groups, such as Hamas. Unlike the PLO, which is largely secular, Hamas is a religious organization. Its members believe the Palestinian cause is a Muslim one. Sheikh Ahmed Yassin founded Hamas in 1987, and militant members soon started attacking Israelis. The group's goal is to form an Islamist state in the Occupied Territories and eventually in all of historic Palestine, ending the existence of Israel. Hamas also organizes charity, offering aid to needy Palestinians. Islamic Jihad is another Islamist Palestinian group. Founded in 1981, the group rose to prominence because of its attacks during the intifada.

killing hundreds, the rest of the world would condemn Israel. If the Palestinians had wielded guns, the IDF wouldn't have hesitated to fire. Instead, in the first year of the intifada, the IDF arrested twenty thousand Palestinians. And the soldiers did fire rubber and sometimes real bullets at the Palestinians when the stone throwing threatened them. Roughly three hundred Palestinians were killed in the first year.

What effects did the intifada have?

FOR THE PALESTINIANS, the intifada was a way to tell Israelis that Palestinians were still a separate people who wanted their own land. It was also a way to convince themselves of the same thing. For the Israelis, the intifada was a rude shock. After years of convincing themselves that the Occupied Territories belonged to them, the Israelis were being reminded by the Palestinians that it wasn't true.

For almost forty years, Israelis had not felt safe. Now the Palestinians inside the Territories were attacking them. The Israelis couldn't feel safe even inside their own country. Many of them resented the Palestinians. Even with the most powerful army in the world, the Israelis could not stop the intifada. Their soldiers were reduced to chasing kids through alleys.

The intifada's effectiveness, however, did not last that long. All of the Palestinians' efforts to boycott, strike, and cause the Israelis economic pain failed, largely because the Israelis were prosperous and could withstand more hardship than the Palestinians could. The Palestinians who quit their jobs eventually asked for them back, desperate to feed their families. The intifada soon became just stone throwing.

But the Palestinians in the Occupied Territories had made it clear to the rest of the world that they wanted their own country. In July 1988, King Hussein of Jordan renounced any Jordanian claim to the West Bank, leaving it to the

Palestinians if Israel ever relinquished control of it. The Palestinians in the Occupied Territories also put pressure on Arafat and the PLO to begin negotiating with the Israeli government for some sort of peaceful resolution. Arafat had long resisted negotiations because he insisted on claiming all of historic Palestine for his people. But many Palestinians in the West Bank and the Gaza Strip wanted a country in what land they had.

In December 1988, under pressure from his people in the Territories, Arafat renounced terrorism and recognized Israel's right to exist, asking the rest of the world to help the Israelis and Palestinians find a two-state solution. Negotiations began between Israel and the PLO, with the United States as moderator. They proceeded slowly for four years.

The most important effect of the intifada was the way it changed the Israeli-Palestinian relationship. Before 1987, the Palestinians in the Territories just accepted the way things were. Afterward, they believed they could have their own country and they felt more like one people. Before 1987, Israelis were able to handle the threat from hostile Arab neighbors and outside Palestinian terrorist groups. They never had to accept the idea of giving up the Occupied Territories. The intifada forced Israelis to consider some important decisions: Should they give up the Territories if that meant peace and an end to the constant threat of attacks? Would giving up the Territories lead to peace or would Palestinians keep fighting until they controlled Israel too? The Israelis and Palestinians are still trying to answer those questions today. But suddenly peace was a possibility.

9.
What was the Oslo peace process?

IN AUGUST 1993, PLO and Israeli leaders shocked the world by announcing they had agreed on the rough outlines of a peace plan during secret negotiations in Oslo, Norway. The Israeli-Palestine Liberation Organization Accord, also known as the Oslo Accord, was finalized with a handshake by Arafat and Israeli Prime Minister Yitzhak Rabin in Washington a month later.

But making peace a reality is a lot harder than agreeing to the idea of peace. Seven years after the Oslo announcement, talks over a final agreement broke down and Palestinians launched a new intifada even bloodier than the first. Both sides bitterly accused each other of betraying the accord.

➔ Why was the Oslo peace agreement possible?

SEVERAL HISTORICAL DEVELOPMENTS led to Oslo. The first hint that peace between the Israelis and Palestinians was possible came in the Camp David Accords between Israel and Egypt, in 1978. The peace set two key precedents: it showed that an Arab nation could recognize Israel, and that Israel was willing to return land it had occupied, the Sinai Peninsula, in exchange for peace and security.

Israeli Prime Minister Yitzhak Rabin shakes hands with Palestine Liberation Organization leader Yasser Arafat, as U.S. President Bill Clinton looks on, September 13, 1993, in Washington, D.C.

During the four years before the Oslo Accord was drafted, the world dramatically changed as the Soviet Union collapsed and Eastern Europeans established democratic governments. The Communist superpower broke into several republics, which meant it would no longer wield major influence in the Middle East. PLO leaders panicked at this development, because the Soviets had traditionally lent them support in international circles such as the United Nations, while America usually backed Israel. Suddenly free from Soviet restrictions on emigration, large numbers of Russian Jews began moving to Israel in a new *aliya*. The Palestinians worried that the Israeli government could move this large wave of Jews into West Bank settlements to take control of more land. The Soviet collapse also made Israelis nervous. With the Cold War over, the United States might not need to back Israel so strongly anymore, because it wouldn't need such a strong anti-Soviet ally in the region.

In August 1990, Iraq, governed by dictator Saddam Hussein, invaded its small neighbor Kuwait. The United States organized a coalition of nations, including several Arab countries, in a liberation mission that became known as the First Gulf War. In January 1991, after months of international talks with Hussein went nowhere, the United States and its allies sent their armies into Kuwait, liberating the Arab nation and pushing Hussein's forces back into Iraq. Seeing the United States cooperate with several Arab nations only increased Israeli fears that Israel was no longer as important an ally to America. The war also affected the Palestinians, because the PLO had supported Hussein, and many Palestinians in Kuwait had welcomed the Iraqi invaders. Many of the Arab nations that fought Iraq were upset at the Palestinians and began cutting back on the financial aid they donated to the PLO.

U.S. president George Bush had promised the Arab nations that he would try to negotiate a peaceful solution to the Israeli-Palestinian conflict if they helped him in the Gulf War. So in 1991, the Israelis, the Palestinians, the United States, and many Arab states sat down in Madrid and began peace negotiations. Later the talks moved to Washington, D.C. But after a year of on-again, off-again talks, the peace process wasn't getting anywhere. In 1992, the government of Norway quietly invited Israeli and Palestinian negotiators to Oslo to hold secret peace talks. Without representatives of other nations and the media watching them, the Israeli and Palestinian negotiators were able to come to an agreement.

➔ What was in the agreement?

THE BASIC IDEA of the accord was that Israel would provide the Palestinians with limited self-rule in the Occupied Territories gradually, over a period of five years. The Palestinians, in return, would recognize Israel and begin working to prevent terrorist attacks against Israelis. Meanwhile, Israeli and Palestinian negotiators would continue talks until both sides agreed to a final settlement on what land the Palestinians would ultimately control, what would happen to Jewish settlements in the Territories, what parts of Jerusalem Palestinians might control, and whether Palestinian refugees would be able to return to their old hometowns in Israel. The idea behind this gradual approach was that both sides would gain trust in each other as each step was implemented, which would help the final negotiations.

Israeli troops handed over control of most of the Gaza Strip and Jericho to the Palestinians' new government, the Palestinian Authority, in May 1994. While the Palestinian Authority built a government in the areas it controlled, negotiators continued to discuss further land transfers. In September 1995, an additional agreement gave the Authority control over more areas. It now completely controlled about 3 percent of the Territories, including all major cities. Israel and the Authority held joint control of villages, about 24 percent of the Territories. The Israelis retained control over the rest of the Territories, including Israeli settlements. Overall, the Palestinian leaders governed 90 percent of the Territories' population, but only 3 percent of the land. Israeli leaders also agreed to give the Palestinians some economic freedom—tax money the Palestinians paid to Israelis was given to the Authority, and Israel began constructing a port near Gaza for the Palestinians to use.

Arafat arrived in Gaza City in July 1994 from Tunis, where he had been living in exile, to a hero's welcome and took power as president of the new Palestinian Authority. Palestinians elected a legislature in 1996. Because Arafat's Fatah Party was the most organized political group in the new Authority, its members quickly took many of the top posts. The Authority adopted the PLO's flag and anthem. The Authority started new radio and TV stations. Courts began hearing cases, though some Palestinians accused the judges of being under Arafat's control.

➜ How did Israelis and Palestinians react to the accords?

A LARGE PORTION of both the Israeli and Palestinian populations supported the agreements, at least initially. After years of violence, the idea of living in peace was attractive. But small yet vocal minorities on both sides opposed the agreements. These opponents did not want to compromise—the Israelis wanted to annex the Occupied Territories as part of a "Greater Israel," and the Palestinians wanted a country in the entire old Mandate of Palestine. Because the Oslo process was gradual and ongoing, opponents on both sides tried to make it impossible for Israeli and Palestinian leaders to negotiate further agreements or a final settlement that would create two separate nations.

Israeli opponents included conservative members of the Likud Party who believed Labor Party prime minister Rabin was rewarding the PLO for terrorism by negotiating with the organization and giving it control of parts of the Territories. Terrorists like Arafat could not be trusted, they argued. The Palestinians were only agreeing to a country for themselves in the Occupied Territories so they could eventually use that land to attack Israel and try to conquer all of it. Some religious Israelis also opposed the accords, arguing that Rabin and the Labor Party were actually disobeying God by giving away part of Eretz Yisrael. Settlers feared that Rabin's government would give all of the Territories to the Palestinians and force the settlers to leave their homes, or worse, that Rabin would pull out Israeli soldiers and refuse to defend the settlers if Palestinians attacked.

This fear drove a few Israelis to violence. They believed violent attacks were the only way to derail what Rabin was doing. On February 25, 1994, just after the Israeli and Palestinian leaders reached an agreement to give the Palestinians control over the Gaza Strip and Jericho, a Jewish settler named Baruch Goldstein walked into the Cave of Patriarchs near Hebron. Jews and Muslims both believe the cave is a holy place, the burial site of six prophets including Abraham and Jacob. The Israeli military controlled the cave and allowed Jews and Muslims to pray there. On that February day, Goldstein pulled out a gun during Muslim prayers and began shooting everyone in sight. Before he was stopped, he had killed twenty-nine Palestinians and wounded many more. Other worshippers tackled him and beat him to death.

Goldstein was a member of the Kach movement, a radical religious Zionist group. His actions were condemned by most Israelis, who were horrified that an Israeli could commit such a violent terrorist act. The Knesset passed tough antiterrorism laws banning Kach. But to many conservative Israelis, Goldstein was a hero. His tombstone in Kiryat Arba was engraved "Here lies the saint, Dr. Baruch Kappel Goldstein, blessed be the memory of the righteous and holy man, may the Lord avenge his blood, who devoted his soul to the Jews, Jewish religion and Jewish land. His hands are innocent and his heart is pure. He was killed as a martyr of God."

Goldstein wasn't the last Israeli opponent of the agreement to commit such a violent act. On November 4, 1995, Rabin spoke at a rally in support of the peace process in Tel Aviv. As he walked to his car, three shots rang out. A young religious student, Yigal Amir, had shot Rabin in the back. The prime minister was rushed to a hospital but died on the operating table. Amir was a religious extremist, who said he killed Rabin because the prime minister had given up the dream of a greater Israel. Investigations showed that some religious Israelis had been urging violent action against Rabin. Some rabbis had actually cited Jewish law to say Rabin had betrayed Israel. The assassination stunned other Israelis. The decades of living with the threat of war and terrorism had always unified Israelis. Now the peace process was revealing divisions that most Israelis had never known existed.

On the Palestinian side, many of the non-Fatah members of the PLO rejected the agreement. Palestinians outside the Territories objected that the question of whether they would be allowed to return to the homes they had fled—an issue referred to as "the right of return"—would not be settled until the final agreement. Islamist groups such as Hamas refused to accept a state in only part of historic Palestine—they wanted all of the Territories and Israel. The most extreme opponents were members of Hamas and Islamic Jihad, who began a series of terrorist attacks on Israel, hoping to antagonize the Israelis enough to end the peace process and begin a full-scale war between Palestinians and Israelis. The two Islamist groups used terrorist attacks with explosives to hit Israel. Their most feared weapon was suicide bombing.

➜ What is suicide bombing?

A SUICIDE BOMBING is an attack committed by someone who knows the explosion will take his own life as well as that of the people he is targeting. Suicide bombers strap explosives such as dynamite to their bodies, and oftentimes other items like nails and ball bearings. The bomber goes to a crowded place and detonates the explosives, killing himself and people around him. The nails, ball bearings, or other metal items become shrapnel, flying through the air and inflicting even more damage. It is one of the most frightening forms of terrorism, because it is very hard to stop a bomber willing to take his own life.

People have committed suicide attacks for almost as long as there have been war and terrorism, because those attacks create so much fear. During the final months of World War II, Japanese pilots called kamikazes would intentionally crash their planes—loaded with gasoline—into American ships, causing huge explosions. In 1980, a Sri Lankan terrorist organization called the Tamil Tigers began a more than twenty-year series of suicide bombings against the Sri Lankan government. In 1983, an Islamist terrorist drove a truck packed with explosives into a building in Beirut, Lebanon, where U.S. Marines were living, killing 241 Americans. The sentry guarding the building later told people that when the truck sped past, the driver smiled at him.

Palestinian terrorist groups have deployed many suicide bombers in the past decade. On April 16, 1993, just a few months before Israel and the PLO announced the Oslo Accord, a Palestinian committed the first suicide bombing of the Israeli-Palestinian conflict. From 1994 to 1996, ten bombers, most sent by Hamas and Islamic Jihad, killed one hundred people.

Why would people kill themselves just so they could kill other people? Some, especially those who have seen their friends or countrymen killed by suicide bombers, argue that the only explanation is that the bombers are evil people. Those who have friends or countrymen who have blown themselves up argue that it is a sign of desperation, that the people who do it feel it is the only way to strike back at a stronger enemy. Complicating the issue is religion. The Qur'an says that those Muslims who die fighting for Islamic causes are guaranteed eternity in paradise with Allah. Once Islamist militants began using suicide bombings against Israel, some Islamic scholars maintained that the attackers were dying for an Islamic cause and therefore were guaranteed a place in paradise. Other scholars argued that all life is precious and Allah doesn't want Muslims killing themselves or others. But to a young Palestinian who lives in fear of Israelis, who doesn't have any job prospects or hope for a better future, the idea of a one-way ticket to paradise might sound tempting.

To Israelis, however, suicide bombing is a horrible weapon, the ultimate terrorist crime. Israelis have very few ways to defend against such attacks. Every public place in Israel suddenly became a target. Many Israelis now try to avoid crowds. When they do go out, they look around for anyone wearing baggy clothing that might conceal explosives. Living under such stress is exhausting.

➜ Why did the Oslo Accords fail?

THE ISLAMIST TERRORISTS' mission to damage the peace process with their suicide attacks worked. A majority of Israelis had supported the idea of giving Palestinians their own country, because the Palestinians promised to end terrorist attacks. But three years after Oslo, terrorists such as Hamas bombers were still killing Israelis. After Rabin's assassination, his foreign minister, Shimon Peres, became prime minister. Peres had personally negotiated portions of the accords with Arafat, so when the terrorism continued, Israelis grew angry with him. In May 1996, Israel held elections. The Likud candidate for prime minister, Binyamin Netanyahu, campaigned by promising to get tough with the Palestinians, vowing he would not give them control of any more land until they stopped the terrorism completely.

Netanyahu won the election. He took office refusing to hand over more land to the Palestinian Authority, even though the accords stipulated he must. Netanyahu also took several steps that upset the Palestinians further. He began an ambitious program of building new settlements in the Territories. In 1990, there were 150,000 settlers in the Territories. Then Netanyahu took over, and by 2000, there were 380,000. Netanyahu's government built roads and infrastructure for these settlements. Netanyahu also authorized construction of a new Jewish neighborhood in East Jerusalem, which Palestinians wanted in the final agreement. In September 1996, Netanyahu allowed archaeologists to open a tunnel under the Temple Mount, sparking fear among Muslims that he was violating sacred Islamic space. Palestinian riots over the decision left forty Palestinians and eleven Israelis dead. Netanyahu seemed to be deliberately provoking the Palestinians.

He certainly made the Palestinians angry. Despite Hamas and Islamic Jihad opposition, a majority of Palestinians had supported the accords initially, even if many had mixed feelings about giving up any claim to Israeli land, which was 78

93

percent of the old Palestine Mandate. But when the Israeli government stopped implementing the accords, the Palestinians began to think the whole peace process was unfair. They saw that the Israelis had made only a partial treaty: The real rewards Palestinians wanted—a complete country in the Territories, economic freedom, a right of return, control of at least part of Jerusalem—would not be negotiated until the final agreement. And Israeli leaders made it clear they expected the Palestinians to compromise on some of those rewards. The Palestinians, on the other hand, had already offered the Israelis everything they wanted in the initial Oslo Accord: recognition of Israel and an end to terrorism. After promising Israel those two things, the Palestinians did not have anything else to offer to get the Israelis to give them what they wanted.

Once most Palestinians decided the accords were unfair, they favored using terrorism to force the Israelis back to the bargaining table. Support for Hamas and Islamic Jihad soared. Arafat couldn't stop the violence. He may have been president of the Palestinian Authority, but he had been living in exile since Israel's founding. There were Palestinian leaders who had been living in the Occupied Territories a lot longer than Arafat, who challenged his control. Some were young Palestinians who had organized the intifada; others were Islamist leaders of Hamas and Islamic Jihad. Arafat worried that if he tried to stop these groups from attacking Israel, the rest of the Palestinians would turn against him.

Arafat's standing was also weakened by his government's corruption. Palestinian Authority accountants at one point estimated that $400 million was disappearing every year from the Authority's budget, money used for bribes or payoffs or to line the pockets of top government officials. Meanwhile, Hamas was funding schools and hospitals for poor Palestinians and doing a better job than the Authority.

When Netanyahu took power and Palestinians turned against the accords completely, Arafat did almost nothing to stop the terrorism. He may have believed the violence would force Netanyahu to make concessions and restart the peace process. But Netanyahu simply retaliated for every Palestinian attack, reimposing many of the harsh rules Palestinians had lived under before the accords. In a vicious cycle, every terrorist attack brought more retaliation, which led to more attacks.

Only four years after the historic agreement in Oslo, Palestinians and Israelis had lost faith in the peace process and trusted each other even less than they had before. Despite attempts by the rest of the world to restart the process, that lack of trust doomed it. U.S. president Bill Clinton in particular made repeated efforts to revive the process. In 1998, he pressured Arafat and Netanyahu into signing a new agreement that would begin gradually implementing the accords again. Netanyahu's conservative supporters were so upset with him for agreeing to sign, that they forced new elections.

Netanyahu lost in the 1999 elections to Labor Party leader Ehud Barak, who promised to negotiate a final agreement that would resolve the conflict once and for all. With Clinton's help, Barak offered a final agreement to Arafat in July 2000. The Palestinian leader rejected it. Arafat claimed Barak did not offer the Palestinians enough land or enough control over Jerusalem. But many observers suspect Arafat rejected the offer because it called for the Israelis to implement the provisions gradually, and Arafat did not trust them to do so. He was also under too much pressure from Palestinians not to accept anything less than 100 percent of what they wanted. Once those talks failed, almost no one believed the Israelis and Palestinians could restart the peace process.

➤ When did the second intifada begin?

WITH THE COLLAPSE of the peace talks, frustration among Israelis and Palestinians was at an all-time high. To have worked so hard and to be even further away from peace made both groups bitter. One small incident could ignite a new wave of violence, just as a random traffic accident sparked the first.

On September 28, 2000, Likud Party leader Ariel Sharon visited al Haram al Sharif, the Noble Sanctuary. Although Israel controls all of Jerusalem, the government allows Muslim Palestinians limited control of the top of the Temple Mount, known as the Noble Sanctuary. Palestinians have long feared Israel would destroy al Aqsa Mosque and the Dome of the Rock and begin building a new Jewish temple. On that September day, Sharon decided to visit the sanctuary to show that Israel still had ultimate control over the sanctuary and all of Jerusalem.

Why is Ariel Sharon such a controversial figure?

HOW COULD PALESTINIANS claim one man's visit to al Haram al Sharif sparked the second intifada? Because Ariel Sharon is one of the most controversial figures in Israeli history. To some people, Sharon is a decorated war veteran and a strong politician dedicated to keeping Israel safe. To others, he is a war criminal and a man bent on killing as many Palestinians as necessary to keep them from having their own country.

Sharon was born in the Palestine Mandate in 1928. Since boyhood, he has been involved in fighting. He joined the Haganah at age fourteen and commanded an IDF platoon during the Israeli War of Independence. When Palestinian fedayeen made cross-border raids in the years after the war, Sharon led a daring group called Unit 101, which would sneak across the border and retaliate against the fedayeen. But some Israelis and Arabs accused the unit of deliberately killing Arab civilians to intimidate the fedayeen. As an officer in the Arab-Israeli wars of 1956, 1967, and 1973, Sharon fought Egyptian forces in the Sinai Peninsula. Several times his leaders praised him for his daring attacks. But they also criticized him for sometimes being more aggressive than necessary. In 1969, he became military commander in charge of the Occupied Territories, and some Israeli officials would later accuse him of being too harsh in his treatment of Palestinians.

The incident that has been the most controversial in Sharon's life, however, took place during the Israeli invasion of Lebanon in 1982. Sharon was defense minister

He said he went as a gesture of peace. But to guarantee his safety, he was escorted by almost one thousand Israeli policemen wearing riot gear.

Palestinians were furious, convinced Sharon was rubbing Israel's control of the third holiest site of Islam in their faces. The next day, after midday prayers, Palestinians began throwing stones from on top of the mount down onto Jews praying at the base of the Western Wall below. Israeli soldiers fired on the rioting Palestinians, killing seven. Palestinians in other parts of Jerusalem started

and planned the campaign. He sent the IDF all the way to Beirut and made the decision to shell the city until the PLO evacuated. His plan worked, forcing the PLO out of the country. But then the Israelis' allies in the war, the Phalangists, who were a Christian-Lebanese militia, sent fighters into the Sabra and Shatila refugee camps, which were home to hundreds of Palestinian refugees. The Phalangist fighters killed hundreds of refugees during the next few days, as retaliation against the PLO, which had been fighting the Christians. IDF soldiers were stationed outside the camps and did nothing to stop the Phalangists. An Israeli government commission investigated the massacres and laid blame mostly with an IDF commander but also blamed Sharon for negligence. Sharon lost his job over the incident,

Israeli Prime Minister Ariel Sharon in his Jerusalem office, May 2004.

and to this day, Palestinians have accused him of being guilty of war crimes.

As prime minister since 2001, Sharon has been no less controversial. Palestinians accuse him of being unwilling to make peace. Sharon and his supporters counter that he will only make peace once all attacks against Israelis stop.

97

rioting too. Within days, Palestinians throughout the Occupied Territories were rioting. It was a new intifada. Palestinians called it al Aqsa intifada, because they claimed Sharon's visit to al Aqsa had triggered it. Sharon and other Israeli leaders alleged that Arafat had been planning a new uprising as a way of forcing Israelis to make more concessions in peace talks, and that Sharon's visit just provided an excuse. There is some truth to both sides' allegations. Sharon's visit was certainly a provocative move, but almost anything could have instigated a new intifada at that time.

➔ How was the second intifada different from the first?

AL AQSA INTIFADA, which was still raging in 2004, was more violent than the first. In the initial two years of fighting alone, 1,800 Palestinians and 570 Israelis died. One factor that made al Aqsa more violent than the first intifada was the increased bitterness and distrust Israelis and Palestinians felt for each other. To many Palestinians, the collapse of the peace process was proof the Israelis were liars who never planned to give them a truly independent country in the Territories. Many believed the Israelis had negotiated only to temporarily stop Palestinian attacks while Israeli settlers grabbed more land in the Territories. To many Israelis, including some who had believed peace was possible, the new intifada was proof of their worst fears: that the Palestinians would never accept anything less than the complete destruction of Israel and the death or expulsion of all Jews.

In 1987, the Palestinians threw stones. In 2000, militants, some of them members of the Palestinian Authority police force, shot at Israeli soldiers with rifles. Suicide bombers attacked Israeli cities with greater frequency and deadlier results. Hamas also fired crude rockets into Israeli towns. The Israelis retaliated with stronger weapons, using tanks and helicopters to attack Palestinian fighters, sometimes killing innocent Palestinians too. In December 2000, the Israeli government started making "targeted killings." Israeli planes or helicopters dropped missiles or bombs on Palestinian militant leaders, usually killing several other Palestinians in the process.

Two televised events early in the fighting stirred up even greater anger among the Palestinian and Israeli people. In the first days of the rioting, a twelve-year-old Palestinian boy named Mohammed al Durrah and his father were caught in a crossfire between fighting Palestinian militants and Israeli soldiers in Jerusalem. Unable to get out of the way, Mohammed was killed and his father badly wounded. The event was caught by a TV cameraman and replayed on Palestinian television for days. Less than a month later, two Israeli reserve soldiers took a wrong turn near Ramallah and ended up at a Palestinian police checkpoint. The police took them to their headquarters. A mob of Palestinians gathered outside, entered the building, and killed the two Israelis. Again, much of the event was caught on video. The Israeli public was horrified and furious.

Barak had tried to contain the violence by closing off the border between Israel and the Territories and cutting off financial aid to the Palestinian Authority, but it did not work. Most Israelis were unhappy with him for his failure at the July peace talks. In February 2001, Israelis elected Sharon prime minister. Sharon promised three things: Israeli settlements would be expanded, Israel would never give up control of any part of Jerusalem, and he would hold no peace talks until all terrorist attacks stopped. Sharon also retaliated more severely against terrorist attacks and more directly against the Palestinian Authority. Each time a Palestinian suicide bomber attacked an Israeli city, Sharon would send tanks or helicopters to strike a Palestinian Authority target such as a police station. He said that if he attacked Arafat's government enough, Arafat would stop the terrorists.

Instead, Arafat supported the terrorists more. By this time, Hamas was so popular with many Palestinians that Arafat couldn't afford not to. Hamas and

Islamic Jihad continued the bombings, and a new group, al Aqsa Martyrs Brigades, which was made up of members of Arafat's Fatah Party, began their own suicide bombings. On March 27, 2002, a suicide bomber detonated his explosives in a hotel in Netanya where Jews were conducting a Passover seder, commemorating the Exodus from Egypt. The bombing killed twenty-nine people.

Sharon responded with Operation Defense Shield, intending to "wipe out the Palestinian infrastructure of terror." Sharon argued that the Palestinian Authority government was just a support organization for terrorists. IDF tanks, soldiers, and helicopters moved into almost every city in the West Bank and began destroying everything the Palestinian Authority had built in seven years. The IDF bulldozed Authority buildings, arrested 8,500 Palestinians, and killed hundreds. The IDF began reoccupying the West Bank cities. For days, the IDF fought militants in the old quarter of the city of Jenin, eventually leveling much of the neighborhood. Their bulldozers also destroyed much of Arafat's headquarters in Ramallah, trapping the leader inside.

More than two years later, this violent cycle continues, despite efforts by the international community to stop it and restart peace talks. Every time it appears the killing has ended, a suicide bomber attacks or the Israeli military kills another Palestinian leader. On an early morning in March 2004, an Israeli missile killed Sheikh Ahmad Yassin, Hamas's leader, as he left a mosque in his wheelchair. Thousands of Palestinians took to the streets to protest, promising suicide bombings in retaliation.

10.
What is life like for Israelis and Palestinians today?

FOR MORE THAN a century, Palestinians and Israelis have lived in conflict with each other. Every day, they share a small piece of land with their bitter enemies. Every day, they confront the possibility that they will see violence and death. Every day, they face the difficult task of wondering how they can end this conflict. The tension has shaped both groups of people dramatically. It has created divisions in both Israeli and Palestinian societies. It has shaped the way the two groups look at each other and themselves. And it has caused a lot of suffering. That is something both Israelis and Palestinians have in common.

➜ How has the conflict shaped Israeli society?

THE EARLY ZIONISTS wanted a homeland so the Jewish people could finally feel safe and free. How painfully ironic that Israelis have built a powerful nation but are consumed with fear. After half a century, Israel is a vibrant country with one of the strongest economies and most powerful militaries in the Middle East. And yet many Israelis are scared to get on a bus because a suicide bomber might detonate explosives and kill everyone on board. Israeli parents worry that their children could be killed by terrorists.

Mordechai and Tzira Schijveschuurder were worried Israeli parents. Motti and Tzila, as their friends called them, were immigrants to Israel, Orthodox Jews, who had moved from the Netherlands to Talmon, a settlement in the West Bank. They had eight children. On August 9, 2001, the couple was taking a day trip to Jerusalem with five of their kids, when a suicide bomber blew himself up outside a Sbarro pizzeria at the corner of Jaffa and King George Streets, the most famous intersection in the city. The blast killed sixteen people, including Motti, Tzila, fourteen-year-old Ra'aya, four-year-old Avraham, and two-year-old Hemda. It wounded the other two daughters. More than one thousand people showed up at the family's funeral, where the bodies were buried in a grove of cypress trees.

Israelis see death all the time. Every May 14, the day before Israelis celebrate the nation's birthday, they remember all the soldiers who died in past battles. Families journey to cemeteries to visit the graves of relatives killed in the wars. The entire nation stops for a moment of silence. Drivers pull their cars over on the highway, get out, and stand in silence to remember the dead. Since the Six-Day War, when Nasser threatened to kill every Jew in the country, most Israelis believe their nation faces the constant threat of another holocaust. Israelis regularly visit memorials to the Holocaust of World War II all around the country. Kids often take field trips to them. Israeli leaders always take foreign leaders to the memorials when they visit Israel. They want to make a point: We are surrounded by enemies, both outside and inside our borders.

All that fear has made it very hard to make peace with the Palestinians. On one hand, Israelis would love to find a solution to the conflict and stop the fighting. On the other, they are scared the Palestinians will not accept peace and will never stop fighting. That concern has divided the Israelis into three groups. Some Israelis believe the conflict is a never-ending war. That's because they believe the Palestinians will never accept anything less than an end to Israel and the death

Israeli soldiers stand guard behind settlers praying close to the Kiryat Arba settlement.

of all Israelis. To those Israelis, making peace is useless. They believe the Palestinians will only use that peace to prepare their fighters to attack Israel again. Because many of those Israelis believe the Palestinians understand only violence, they want to use hard methods against them. They feel the IDF should use its superior military force to kill Palestinian terrorists, the government should punish average Palestinians with strict rules until the terrorism stops, and settlers should move onto as much land in the Occupied Territories as possible so Israel can hold on to it.

Some Israelis believe the opposite. They think Israelis will not have peace until they make as fair an agreement as possible with the Palestinians. Even if terrorism continues, they believe, Israeli leaders should keep talking with the Palestinian leaders to try and find a fair solution. The IDF should use more defensive measures to stop the terrorists from attacking Israel. The Israeli government should improve economic and living conditions in the Occupied Territories so Palestinians are less motivated to attack. And the government should force the settlers to stop building more settlements and instead move back to Israel proper.

Most Israelis, however, are torn between those two camps. They want to make peace with the Palestinians. Almost 50 percent of Israelis supported the idea of a separate Palestinian country in 2001, even though the Palestinians had already begun the second intifada. But they also want to be safe, and they worry about whether the Palestinians can be trusted. The new intifada has hardened Israelis' opinions of the Palestinians. The majority of Israelis want them to stop all terrorism before negotiations begin. Also they disagree with many Palestinian demands. They may support the idea of a Palestinian country, but they don't support giving up any part of Jerusalem and they don't support a right of return.

All these different opinions have made it hard for Israelis to find a solution to the conflict. Until they can agree with one another about what their nation wants, they will not be able to make peace.

➔ How else are Israelis divided?

ISRAELIS' INTERNAL DISAGREEMENTS about how to solve their conflict with the Palestinians are complicated by many other divisions in their society. Israel may be a tiny country, but its population is very diverse. About 80 percent is Jewish Israeli, but because the Jews who founded or immigrated to Israel are from all over the world, they bring many different customs and beliefs with them. Some are Ashkenazic Jews, whose ancestors lived in northern Europe. Others are Sephardic, descended from Jews who lived in Spain, Portugal, and the Middle

East. These groups have different beliefs, and they don't always get along. If you asked four Israelis what a Jew is, you might get four different answers. Different Jewish Israelis believe different things about what Judaism means, about what kind of country Israel should be, and about how Israelis should treat the Palestinians.

About half of Jewish Israelis are secular Jews, which means they do not actively practice their religion, believing instead that their Judaism is a heritage or ethnicity. Most of Israel's founders were secular. Because many of the laws and customs of Judaism were developed in the Diaspora as a way of reminding Jews that they were a different people, secular Jews believe those laws and customs are not necessary now that they live in Israel. They walk down Jewish streets, buy things with shekels, and speak in Hebrew. Why do they need to keep kosher?

A little fewer than a third of Jewish Israelis are more religious than secular Jews and believe in Orthodox Judaism but not in the much stricter ultra-Orthodox practices. These Jews don't see living in Israel as a substitute for going to synagogue every Saturday for Sabbath.

About 15 percent of Israeli Jews are ultra-Orthodox, non-Zionist Jews, most of whom are known as Haredim. Their strict form of Judaism requires keeping all 613 Jewish laws, including specific ways of dressing, eating, and praying. The non-Zionists do not worry about Israel being a Jewish state, because they believe only God can reestablish a Jewish kingdom in Israel. If Turks or Arabs still governed the land, that would be fine with the non-Zionists. They live in their own communities, and they don't like it if less observant Jews move in. The non-Zionists serve in the Knesset and government posts. They may not support the idea of a Jewish state, but since Israel is one, they want it to have laws that encourage a strict interpretation of Jewish rules.

About 5 percent of Jewish Israelis are both ultra-Orthodox and Zionist, and are known as the Haredi-Leumi. These ultra-Orthodox Zionists believe that Israel's founding as a Jewish state was an event of biblical importance, a key first step before God sends the Messiah to save the world. Because of that, they believe all of Eretz Yisrael is sacred ground. They are the most opposed to the idea of giving the Palestinians a country. They have also been the leaders of many settlement groups, establishing communities such as Kiryat Arba.

These different groups of Israelis even send their children to different schools. Secular Jewish children attend secular public schools, while Orthodox Jewish children go to religious public schools. Children of Haredim and Haredi-Leumi attend private religious schools called yeshivas.

Military service is a controversial issue in Israel. The nation's strong military is a major reason the country has survived several wars and terrorist attacks during its brief history. Israelis are required to serve in the military—three years for men and two to three for women—and after that, they become reservists until they are forty-five, serving one month of each year. There are exemptions, however. Women can opt out of service if they claim they are religiously observant. (Most do not.) Arab Israelis are not required to serve, though some do, particularly members of the Druze community. Most controversially, many ultra-Orthodox Jews do not serve. When Israel was founded, Ben-Gurion made a deal with the chief ultra-Orthodox rabbi: In exchange for the rabbi supporting the new government, Ben-Gurion allowed the rabbi to set religious rules for the new country. Also, the government would exempt a group of "religious scholars" from military service. In 1948, there were four hundred such scholars. By the 1990s, there were 32,000. This has caused conflict with some secular Israelis, who ask why the non-Zionists should have a say on what food restaurants are allowed to serve or whether public transportation can operate on Saturdays or even how people get married, when they won't serve in the military.

→ Who are the Arab Israelis?

ABOUT 20 PERCENT of Israel's total population is Arab Israeli. The Arab Israelis are Palestinians who remained in Israel proper after its founding, and most of them are Muslim, though others are Christian or Druze. Life was hard for Arab Israelis in the initial years after the Israeli War of Independence. The government did not trust them, so it required them to live in certain areas controlled by the military and limited their travel.

Today the government has promised to treat Arab Israelis as equal citizens, but they still face discrimination. In 1992, the Knesset adopted a series of laws to guarantee civil rights for all Israelis, but also to again define Israel as a Jewish state. In 1995, an Arab couple named Adel and Iman Qa'adan tried to buy a plot for a home in the Jewish settlement town of Katzir. The town clerk refused, saying the law forbade him to sell that land to non-Jews. They took him to court. On March 8, 2000, the Israeli Supreme Court ruled that discrimination against Arab Israeli citizens was illegal. But it did not order the clerk to sell the couple the land they wanted. In 2002, the Knesset tried to pass a law banning Arab purchases of Jewish lands, for security purposes. The government withdrew the bill after being compared to South Africa's apartheid regime, which treated blacks as second-class citizens. Arab Israelis do serve in the Knesset.

Many Arab Israelis feel isolated. On one hand, they are citizens of Israel, and most—93 percent in a 1995 survey—recognize it as a legitimate country. But they are related to Palestinians, and are upset by the memory of how Israel took control of most of the old Palestine Mandate. They are split over whether they should support the Palestinian cause. Most have been wary of supporting terrorist tactics. In 1988 and 2000, large numbers of Arab Israelis marched in the streets to show solidarity with the Palestinians in the Occupied Territories. This sparked fear and resentment among Jewish Israelis, who suddenly worried the Arabs were not really loyal citizens and would help the Palestinians attack Jews.

➜ How has the conflict shaped Palestinian society?

PALESTINIANS ALSO LIVE in fear—the fear that they could be arrested or killed by Israeli soldiers or settlers at any moment. But there is also a more long-term fear—the fear that their lives will never improve. Because of the occupation and the endless fighting, the Palestinians live in poor conditions, with no hope of a brighter economic future. Every day, they are surrounded by things that remind them that they do not have their own country. All these things make them feel they have no control over their lives.

Today more than 50 percent of Palestinians in the Occupied Territories live in poverty. Many live in squalid refugee camps with no access to clean water. One camp near Gaza City with hundreds of residents has nine bathrooms for all of them. Because Israel controls their economy, many Palestinians have to go into Israel to work. Before the second intifada began, 140,000 Palestinians crossed the border each day. Now Israel's government allows only 30,000 to 50,000 across. Many days it doesn't allow anyone to cross, which means those Palestinians don't work and don't earn money to feed their families.

The Israelis make the Palestinians who do want to cross the border, or even just travel from one Palestinian town to another, stand in long lines at military checkpoints, waiting for soldiers to search them to make sure they are not carrying explosives. Since cars cannot go through the checkpoints, some Palestinians take cabs to the checkpoints, get out, walk across, and then hop in another cab. Or they walk. Meanwhile, bypass roads allow Jewish settlers to quickly drive through the Territories. Palestinians sometimes throw rocks at their cars.

Israeli troops invade West Bank towns and search houses without warning. They do not ring the doorbell, instead bursting in with guns drawn. The army can impose curfews under which no Palestinian can leave his or her house, sometimes for days at a time. Israeli planes and helicopters target the homes of terrorist leaders, usually killing a few other Palestinians as well during the attack. The IDF destroys the houses of suicide bombers' families, forcing the residents to move out with just a few minutes' notice. On rare occasions, Palestinians have refused to leave their homes and have been crushed when the buildings collapse. The Israeli government restricts construction of new houses.

For almost a century now, Palestinians have felt a sense of helplessness. At the same time, they have developed a national identity. Because of their conflict with the Israelis and their fruitless struggle to gain their own country, Palestinians' national identity is largely about victimhood. For Israelis, the key moment in their history is the War of Independence, when their brave fighters secured a new nation. For Palestinians, the key moment in their history is also the Israeli War of Independence, but for many of them that war was about fleeing from their homes into exile.

Much of what they believe now centers on their hatred of Israel and their dream of returning to old villages they lived in before the 1948 war. Victimhood motivates almost everything they do as a people. Palestinian leaders spend an enormous amount of time and effort trying to tell the rest of the world how much they are suffering under Israeli rule. That sense of victimhood has even allowed them to send young men and women to kill themselves for the Palestinian cause.

⇒ How has terrorism changed Palestinian society?

ON WALLS THROUGHOUT the West Bank and the Gaza Strip, there are posters of suicide bombers who have killed themselves and Israelis. These posters look like the images of musicians and sports stars that American kids put on their walls. Palestinian children are told that these suicide bombers are heroic martyrs to be looked up to. Songs and poems pay tribute to them. Parents of martyrs receive money from charities. Many Palestinian children tell people they dream of becoming martyrs one day.

Hiba Daraghmeh was nineteen in 2003, a student learning English at al Quds University. Two years earlier, her brother Bakr, a member of a Palestinian security force, was shot during a gun battle with Israeli troops. Later, Israelis arrested him, searched the family home, and eventually sentenced Bakr to twenty-two years in prison. Hiba was furious. One day in May 2003, she walked into a shopping center in the Israeli town of Afula and blew herself up, killing two others and wounding seventy. She was the first female suicide bomber, and her family is still paying the price. Israeli troops knocked down the family's home in Jenin, and

An Israeli soldier passes a martyr poster for Palestinian woman suicide bomber Hiba Daraghmeh.

Hiba's mother had no place to go. Now the only picture she has of her daughter is a poster printed by Islamic Jihad to commemorate Hiba's attack.

To much of the rest of the world, terrorism is a crime. But to Palestinians, it has become an accepted way to fight. Israelis fight Palestinians with tanks, planes, and helicopters. Palestinians don't have those things. That makes this an unfair fight in their eyes. Instead, they have nineteen-year-olds willing to strap dynamite to their bodies and kill themselves and others. Israeli children revere war heroes. Palestinians see their martyrs as war heroes. Terrorism is the only thing that has gotten the world to pay attention to the Palestinian cause. But the price of using terrorism is great.

➔ What do Palestinians want?

PALESTINIAN SOCIETY IS split, just like Israeli society, on what is the best solution to this conflict. A major reason Palestinians could not make the Oslo peace process succeed is because they are still not sure what they want. On one hand, Palestinians want to live in peace, and many are ready to accept a country in the Occupied Territories. But even those who want that aren't sure what the specifics should be. Some want all of Jerusalem to be the Palestinian country's capital. Others would accept just East Jerusalem, while others would accept the United Nations controlling Jerusalem. Some of the Palestinians worry that a country in the Occupied Territories would be too economically dependent on Israel and want measures to prevent that. Some want every Jewish settlement removed from the Territories. Others would accept some larger settlements remaining under Israeli control if Israeli leaders gave the Palestinians an equal amount of land across the border in Israel as compensation.

On the other hand, many Palestinians refuse to make peace until all refugees who fled villages in what is now Israel are allowed to return to those villages. This demand for the right of return is not realistic. The villages are gone. Israelis have built towns on top of them or let their buildings rot. Israel will never accept millions of Palestinians moving into Israel. But the pain of abandoning those villages has made it too hard for Palestinians to let go of the dream of returning. After all, it was only five decades ago that they lived in those towns. Many Palestinians still carry keys from their houses in those abandoned villages. The keys are reminders of what they left behind. What's more, there are many Palestinians who want nothing less than all of the old Palestine Mandate and some will not be satisfied until all Israelis leave the Holy Land.

The majority of Palestinians can't decide among these options. Until they can settle on a common vision of what their country should be, they will not be able to make peace with Israel. They will continue being victims.

➤ How do Israelis and Palestinians see each other?

ISRAELI PRIME MINISTER Golda Meir once said there are no Palestinians. Arafat said many times that the Jews are just a religious group; there is no such thing as an Israeli. A leading reason Palestinians and Israelis find it hard to make peace is that neither one accepts the other's legitimacy.

When IDF soldiers invaded parts of Beirut in 1982, one building they went into was a PLO archive containing historical documents such as deeds to houses Palestinians owned in old villages now in Israel. This archive was the PLO's effort to prove Palestinians were a distinct people. The IDF soldiers confiscated all the documents and defaced the archive, writing on one wall, "Palestinian? What is a Palestinian?" Many Israelis today still claim that Palestinians are no different from any other Arabs. That means they have no legitimate claim to land in the old Palestine Mandate. Some Israelis have even suggested a "peace plan" under which all Palestinians would leave the Occupied Territories and move to Jordan, or some other Arab country. Israel would then annex the Territories. Israeli textbooks stress that the term Palestinian wasn't widely used until the 1950s.

On the other side, many Palestinians refuse to admit Israelis have any real connection to the Holy Land. Palestinian religious leaders have issued statements saying there is no proof a Jewish temple ever stood on the Temple Mount. The whole idea is a fabrication, they say, to give the Jews a claim to Palestinian land. Palestinians say Zionism is not about Jews returning to their homeland, but a racist plan to conquer the Middle East and the world.

All of this, of course, is nonsense. No matter how Palestinian nationalism developed, there's no denying it now exists. No matter how Israel was founded, there's no denying it now exists. When Palestinians and Israelis deny each other's legitimate claims to the Holy Land, that makes it

What are Israeli and Palestinian children taught about each other?

AFTER THE OSLO Accords, the Palestinian Authority took control of schools in the Occupied Territories. Israelis became quite upset when they found out what the Palestinians were teaching their children. Textbooks in the schools showed maps of Israel labeled "Palestine." The books taught that there is one big piece of land called Palestine, and made no mention that 78 percent of it is Israel. Palestinian children also learn routinely about brave martyrs who kill Jews. Many learn that Jews are bloodthirsty, evil creatures descended from pigs, and that Allah hates them.

Israeli schools teach a less biased curriculum, but it has problems too. Less noble events in Israeli history, such as the massacre at Deir Yassin, are played down or ignored. The textbooks often refer to Palestinians as Arabs, refusing to call them a distinct people. Israeli children's books from earlier decades are still popular, even though they usually portray Arabs as crafty, deceitful, and savage. Israeli children routinely hear how horrible Palestinian terrorists are, but hear almost nothing about Israeli terrorists like Baruch Goldstein.

easier not to make peace. It also makes it easier to use violence against each other. If they believe their enemies are evil outsiders trying to steal their land, it's easier to justify killing them.

During the 1990s, while the peace process was still alive, some Israelis began to change their attitudes. Israeli historians published books taking a real look at who the Palestinians are and how Israel was founded. Some books examined the Israeli War of Independence and admitted that the Israelis had used force and intimidation to make Palestinians flee their villages. These historical studies forced many Israelis to reevaluate their opinions of Palestinians. Some Israelis began to question the harsh occupation measures their government was using in the Territories. Unfortunately, few Palestinians took similar steps to change their views of Israelis.

No matter how the Israeli-Palestinian conflict is resolved, these two peoples are going to be sharing the same small piece of land. They will have to learn to live together, even if it is in two separate countries. Al Aqsa intifada was just the latest of the attempts made by both sides to wipe each other out, and it has not worked. It has only revealed that unless both sides agree on a solution to their conflict, neither side can live in peace. The one thing both Palestinians and Israelis want most of all is recognition. They each want the other side to say, You are a legitimate people and you have a valid claim to this land.

11

How has the rest of the world responded to the conflict?

PEOPLE IN THE West and the Middle East pay a lot of attention to the Israelis and Palestinians, even though there are many other ethnic conflicts in the world today, several of which are more deadly. As we discussed earlier, a big reason for the focus on Israel and the Occupied Territories is that most people in the West and Middle East see Israel and the Occupied Territories as holy land. In China or Japan, where there are few Christians, Muslims, or Jews, the news rarely talks about what happens in Israel. But the Western half of the world is focused on Israel, and the conflict there has had a major impact on relations among America, Europe, and the Middle East.

→ How has the United States responded to the conflict?

THE UNITED STATES has been Israel's most loyal ally almost since Zionists founded the Jewish state. Israel was a major friend to America in the Middle East during the Cold War. America sends Israel large amounts of military and financial aid each year (it also sends aid to other Middle Eastern allies), and more tourists from America visit Israel than any other Middle Eastern country, giving money to its economy.

America and Israel haven't always agreed on every issue. During the Jewish nation's early years, the U.S. government hesitated to provide the military aid the Israelis wanted, for fear of upsetting Arab nations, although U.S. leaders eventually changed their minds. The United States opposed Israel's 1956 invasion of Egypt, worried that the Soviet Union would get involved and the United States would have to protect Israel. In 1985, the U.S. government discovered that one of its own intelligence analysts, Jonathan Pollard, had been passing state secrets to the Israelis. Pollard was arrested and sentenced to life in prison, a punishment Israel objects to. Overall, however, most Americans today see Israel as an ally, and they support the United States' alliance with Israel because it is a familiar friend.

Israel supporters chant during a rally in front of the U.S. Capitol in Washington, D.C., April 2002. Thousands of people from around the country gathered to show solidarity with Israelis.

One reason Americans trust Israel is that it has a democratic government, as the United States does. Religion is another reason. The majority of Americans are Christians, and many of them believe that what happens in Israel and the Occupied Territories, the land where they believe Jesus Christ lived and died and where he will return when the world comes to an end, is important to their religion. For some American Christians, that just means following news in the region and praying for peace. But for others, it means trying to have a direct influence on the conflict. Evangelical Christians, Protestants who believe in a strict interpretation of the Bible, argue that the Israelis must have America's full support. They interpret passages of the New Testament to mean that Jews must rebuild the temple in Jerusalem before Jesus can return to Earth. Many believe Israelis must keep control of all of Eretz Yisrael. Evangelical Christian organizations have lobbied the U.S. government to stand more strongly behind the Israelis and not push for a peace treaty with the Palestinians.

America is home to the largest Jewish population in the world, and many American Jews have urged their government to support Israel no matter what happens during the conflict with the Palestinians. American Jews are also an important source of financial aid and tourism money for Israel. The Israelis encourage this by lobbying the U.S. government for support and buying advertisements in the United States urging Americans to visit Israel. Many Israelis believe that, because their country has so many enemies, they must keep the United States on their side.

Because Israel is the Jewish homeland, many Jews all over the world, including Americans Jews, see it as a symbol of Judaism. When Israel is strong and prosperous, they believe it is good news for all Jews. For that reason, many American Jews back Israel in the conflict and are its most loyal supporters. During al Aqsa intifada, when President George W. Bush made a rare plea for Sharon's government to restart peace talks, Jewish and Evangelical Christian American supporters held a huge protest in Washington. Bush has consistently backed the Israelis since then, calling on Palestinians to end terrorism and remove Arafat from power before peace talks can resume.

But a few Jewish Americans are disappointed with Israeli actions in the conflict. Because they see Israel as a symbol of Judaism, they don't like it when its government uses oppressive measures against the Palestinians. Some Israelis react angrily to this, responding that Israel is just a country trying to defend itself, not a symbol of Judaism. Yet, when those Israelis lobby pro-Israel American Jews and Evangelical Christians for support, they emphasize its identity as the Jewish homeland.

The terrorist attacks of September 11, 2001, only strengthened the ties between Israel and America. Americans learned what it was like to be the victims of terrorism and felt more sympathy for Israelis, who had lived with the threat of terror for years. Sharon saw this as an opportunity to win more American support for his harsh counterstrikes against the Palestinians. He began calling Israel's fight against Palestinian terrorists just another front in America's war on terrorism, and called Arafat the Palestinian Osama bin Laden. When the Israeli military killed the leader of Hamas in 2004, Sharon called him the Palestinian bin Laden too. All of this ignored the fact that Palestinian terrorists and al Qaeda terrorists have very different goals: the Palestinians are trying to gain their own nation whereas al Qaeda's members are attacking a nation thousands of miles away because they hope to incite a world war between Muslims and the United States.

The Palestinians have had little luck appealing to Americans for support. They have never had a country of their own, so America hasn't needed an alliance with them. The Palestinian-American and Arab-American communities are relatively new and have become politically active only in recent years. University studies have found that most Americans don't actually know why the Palestinians are fighting with the Israelis. While Americans can sympathize with Israeli victims of terrorist attacks after 9/11, most cannot know what life is like for the Palestinians in the Occupied Territories. And the Palestinians' use of terror has alienated most Americans from their cause.

⇥ How has Europe responded to the conflict?

WHILE MOST AMERICANS have little sympathy for Palestinians, most Europeans have little sympathy for Israelis. In opinion polls conducted by European journalists, most Europeans think Palestinians deserve a homeland and believe the Israelis are too harsh in the methods they use against the Palestinians.

This is a recent development, however. In the first two decades after Israel's creation, most major European nations supported Israel. Many Europeans felt guilty that they had not stopped the Holocaust before the Nazis killed 6 million Jews. From 1948 to 1967, European media coverage of Israel focused on how strong and able the new nation was. In some way, Europeans may have been trying to convince themselves that the Jews were okay; that Europe did not need to keep punishing itself for the Holocaust.

But since the 1967 war, European views of Israel have worsened. Most Europeans disapprove of Israel's occupation of the West Bank and Gaza Strip, and some have loudly protested the measures the Israeli government has used against the Palestinians. It's unclear why European leaders seem to expect a higher standard of behavior from Israel than from other Middle Eastern nations. They focus much more attention on the Israeli government's actions than on those of far harsher regimes in the Middle East.

There are fewer Jews in Europe today than there were a century ago, thanks to emigration and the Holocaust. But the number of Arab-Europeans has skyrocketed in the past twenty years, as Arabs have left the Middle East to escape poverty and repressive regimes. These Arab-Europeans share the same view of Israel as many Arabs in the Middle East. They have been outspoken opponents of Israel's control over the Occupied Territories. When the second intifada began, there were a disturbing number of anti-Semitic incidents in Europe, including attacks on synagogues, and Israeli leaders complained that European governments were not doing enough to protect European Jews. Europe and Israel appear to be growing further apart.

➤ How has the Middle East responded to the conflict?

THE STRUGGLE BETWEEN the Israelis and Palestinians has had a dramatic effect on the rest of the Middle East. It has also affected relations between the nations of the Middle East and the West, particularly the United States. Because most Zionist settlers were European Jews, many Arabs believe they were merely colonists, taking over Palestine for Europe. There would be no Israel if Great Britain and France hadn't conquered the Ottoman Empire and if Britain hadn't decided to create a homeland for Jews in Palestine. To understand why Arab hostility toward Israel remains so high, it's important to also remember that most Arab nations were European colonies until the middle of the twentieth century.

Many Middle Eastern people have now shifted their hostile attitude away from Europe and toward the United States. The United States did not colonize the Middle East as Britain and France did, but it has been deeply involved in the region during the Cold War and the war on al Qaeda, building strategic alliances with Middle Eastern leaders. The second Gulf War, in which America and its allies invaded Iraq, overthrew Saddam Hussein, and began working with Iraqis to create a new government, has only solidified Arab public opinion that the United States is trying to control the region. In light of their resentment and fear of the West, many Arabs look at Israel, which was established by Europeans and receives crucial support from America, as nothing more than a Western colony, built on the third holiest city in Islam.

A Jordanian man burns the American flag during a rally in Amman, Jordan, April 2004.
Hundreds of Jordanians gathered outside the capital's al Yarmuk mosque to show solidarity
with Palestinians under Israeli occupation.

Arab leaders have often encouraged this attitude. Many people in the Middle
East live in poverty. Some live under repressive regimes, which use torture to
discourage dissent. Some of these governments owe their power to the West.
Jordan's king is the great-grandson of an Arabian prince put on the throne by
Britain. The Saudi royals are close American allies. To counter the perception
that they are pawns of the West, many Arab rulers encourage or allow anger and
hostility toward Israel. They prefer for their subjects to be angry at Israelis
rather than at them. Arab governments also openly tolerate or even encourage
anti-Semitism. Egyptian television, which is controlled by the government,
showed a miniseries in 2003 based on the Protocols of the Elders of Zion, alleging
that the anti-Semitic fabrication was fact.

121

Are Arab nations encouraging Palestinian terrorism?

ISRAEL AND THE United States have long complained that Arab leaders have not condemned Palestinian terrorism more strongly. But many Arabs, like Palestinians, see terrorism in this conflict as a legitimate tactic to be used against a militarily superior enemy. The subject has created great tension between the United States and Middle Eastern nations, especially as President Bush has regularly called the war against al Qaeda a war against all terrorism. He has also used the phrase "homicide bombers" to describe suicide bombers, complaining that the original term doesn't make it clear enough that these terrorists are killing other people. Arab leaders prefer to say that they dislike attacks by both sides, thus condemning violence committed by both Palestinians and Israelis.

Israelis have accused Arab leaders of encouraging suicide bombers. Islam requires all Muslims to make regular charitable donations called *zakat*. Some Arab countries actually collect *zakat* through taxes. The money raised is often given to Palestinian charity organizations. Some use the money to help ease Palestinian poverty; others give the money to families of suicide bombers. Israel has accused Arab leaders of doing this to encourage Palestinians to become bombers, because the bombers know their families will receive financial aid. While Saddam Hussein was still the leader of Iraq, he directly paid suicide bombers' families $25,000 each in the hope that Arabs would see him as a sympathetic figure. When the United States began Gulf War II to depose Hussein, President Bush argued that removing Hussein would weaken support for Palestinian terrorists and force their leaders to stop their attacks and resume negotiations with Israelis. That has not happened so far.

➔ Why does it matter how the rest of the world sees this conflict?

ALL THE ATTENTION the West and Middle East give to the Israeli-Palestinian conflict raises some difficult questions. Every night, television news broadcasts images of the conflict into homes around half the world. American news anchors talk of the latest suicide bombing and how many Israeli lives it claimed. Arab news channel reporters show Israeli tanks and helicopters retaliating against Palestinians. All of this makes people in America and the Middle East even more upset about the conflict, more supportive of the side they agree with, and more angry at the side they oppose. It's possible that all this attention paid to an ethnic conflict in one tiny country is making the conflict worse by encouraging both sides not to back down.

On the other hand, American and Arab leaders have great influence with Israeli and Palestinian leaders. They could urge both sides to sit down and try to negotiate a new peace agreement. But American and Middle Eastern leaders should not overestimate their influence. Israelis and Palestinians must truly agree with each other if they are to make a lasting peace.

12.
Why is peace so hard?

THERE IS NO simple answer to that question. Many Israelis, Palestinians, and people all over the world have asked it already. Understanding why there is a conflict between Israelis and Palestinians does not make it easy to find a solution to the struggle. It only raises more complicated questions.

→ How has each side's fear made the peace process difficult?

ISRAELIS' AND PALESTINIANS' fears make it almost impossible for them to trust one another and negotiate a successful peace. The Oslo Accords failed because neither side had enough faith in the other to set its fears aside. No one wants to live in perpetual conflict, but many Palestinians and Israelis worry that any agreement will make life worse than it is now. When Egyptian president Anwar Sadat wanted to negotiate with the Israelis in 1977, he made the bold move of traveling to Jerusalem and recognizing Israel. No Arab leader had done that, and it earned Israelis' trust. No Palestinian or Israeli leader has made such a bold move to convince the other side that they are negotiating in good faith.

→ Why can't Israelis and Palestinians compromise?

SOME PALESTINIANS AND Israelis still believe they can win this conflict. They believe if they only inflict enough pain on their enemies, they can make their enemies give in to their demands. Other Israelis and Palestinians believe they can't win, but they also can't afford to lose. They would rather fight endlessly than compromise. A lasting peace treaty would force both the Palestinians and Israelis to make difficult choices they don't want to make. The Israelis might have to force West Bank and Gaza Strip settlers to move back to Israel. Palestinian leaders might have to tell Palestinians that they will have to give up any claim to land in Israel proper.

Also, both sides would have to recognize each other's legitimacy. Israeli leaders might have to acknowledge to Palestinians that their nation unfairly forced Palestinians to leave their villages during the Israeli War of Independence. Palestinian leaders might have to admit that the Jews lived in the Holy Land in ancient times and thus have a real connection to the land. Israelis and Palestinians are so bitter at each other after a century of fighting that they find that impossible.

→ Is it possible the conflict could stop without a peace agreement?

After years of frustrating failures at negotiation, it's understandable that each side would like to simply force the other to accept peace terms. In 2002, the Israeli government took actions that suggested it was trying to impose its own version of peace. Ariel Sharon's government began building a barrier around the West Bank. Sharon and other Israeli leaders call it a security fence, and portions of it

A Palestinian boy walks next to the Israeli "security barrier," on the edge of Jerusalem, February 2004.

are made from wire fencing and barbed wire. But other portions, those that run through highly populated areas, are made from concrete wall sections more than twenty feet high. The Israelis claim they are building it to prevent terrorists from sneaking around checkpoints to attack Israeli civilians. The barrier, however, is not being constructed on the exact border of the West Bank. Instead, the barrier will curve in and out of the West Bank, sometimes going miles inside it. Members of Sharon's government claim these detours are necessary so that the barrier will protect Jewish settlements. But in many places, the barrier cuts through land the Palestinians hope to call their own someday. Farmers have been separated from their fields, children from their schools, and families from their relatives. The Israelis have set up checkpoints where Palestinians can pass through the barrier, but these are miles apart and open only at limited times.

Some Palestinians suspect Israel is trying to draw a new border. The Israelis and Palestinians have never agreed to the exact borders of a Palestinian state, but many people have assumed it would follow the borders that existed before the Six-Day War, with maybe a few changes to put a handful of large settlements inside Israel and compensate the Palestinians with other land. But in November 2003, Sharon announced that because he could not negotiate with Palestinian leaders, he planned to withdraw settlers and soldiers gradually, first from the Gaza Strip and then from small parts of the West Bank, letting the Palestinians figure out their own government. He is drawing borders without negotiations. In April 2004, U.S. president George W. Bush helped Sharon by endorsing the idea and saying America accepted that Israel would retain control over parts of the West Bank where there are large settlements. Until that moment, America's official view of settlements was that they were "an obstacle to peace." Bush also said Palestinians need to give up the right of return for there to be peace. Decades earlier when Sharon had promoted building settlements in the Territories, he said it would help Israel hold on to that land forever. He may be proving himself right.

→ Why would Israel unilaterally withdraw?

Sharon's proposal to unilaterally withdraw from the Territories took many people by surprise. Many of his fellow conservatives strongly oppose giving up any land, but he may believe it is necessary for Israel's survival. In a few decades, the Arab Israelis and Palestinians will outnumber Jewish Israelis. If that happens, Palestinians might stop asking for their own country and instead ask Israel to annex the Territories and make them Israeli citizens, with the right to vote.

That would put Israelis in a bind. If they refused to make the Palestinians full citizens, Israel would no longer be a democracy. The Palestinians could claim Israel was no better than South Africa under apartheid. Before the 1990s, a white minority ruled South Africa and blacks were second-class citizens without the right to vote. Much of the rest of the world protested against apartheid in the 1980s, boycotting South Africa. Finally, the white government caved in and gave blacks the right to vote. Those new black voters elected a black government. If Palestinians became Israeli citizens, they could vote and elect a government that could declare Israel a non-Jewish state. Sharon may be trying to avoid that by building a wall and declaring anything inside it a Palestinian state.

It's possible that Sharon's plan could lead to peace—in the summer of 2004, some Gazans hoped a withdrawal would allow them to reform their local government. But Palestinians will probably reject a peace they did not agree to. Arafat's death in November 2004 left them without a clear leader who can speak for all Palestinians while trying to negotiate a lasting peace with Israel.

➤ If the Israeli and Palestinian leaders did make peace, could it last?

JUST BECAUSE LEADERS make an agreement does not mean their people change their own opinions. For decades, Palestinians and Israelis have seen each other as enemies. That fear of each other has colored how they have lived their lives. Both sides would have to learn to live together. For Israelis and Palestinians to live in peace, they would have to work at understanding each other.

What is Seeds of Peace?

"TREATIES ARE NEGOTIATED by governments—peace is made by people." That saying comes from one group trying to change minds. For several years now, a few hundred kids from Israel, the Occupied Territories, and Arab nations have attended summer camp in the woods of Maine in the Seeds of Peace program. This organization brings the children together with staff members experienced in building relationships so they can learn what it is like to live together, to see that their "enemy" is human, and to develop trust and respect. Once kids finish the program, they can keep in touch with each other back in their native countries. The program has been successful enough that other nations with long conflicts have sent children. Groups in Israel have started similar programs.

First-grade pupils show off their artwork in their class at the Bilingual School, November 2002. In each class half the pupils are Jewish and half are Arab, and classes are team-taught by two teachers, one Jewish and one Arab.

➔ Is peace impossible?

ONE OBSTACLE TO peace is that after decades of conflict and the failure of the Oslo peace process, many people on both sides and in the rest of the world believe that peace is impossible. The world is full of places that were once torn apart by conflict and are now peaceful, however. While some individuals favor violence, the majority of Israelis and Palestinians want to live in peace. Finding a solution requires believing peace is possible. Until both sides believe that, they can refuse to make the tough choices and sacrifices that are necessary for peace.

➤ What can you do?

THIS BOOK IS just a beginning. Try to learn more about Israelis, Palestinians, the Middle East, and other parts of the world by reading more books. Follow the news on television, in magazines and newspapers, and on the Internet. Ask your teachers lots of questions. Remember that there's no such thing as the "right" opinion on such a difficult subject. Everyone has a different point of view, so listen respectfully to other people's because each one can provide a new perspective on this conflict. Learn more about Judaism, Christianity, and Islam. Explore new languages like Hebrew and Arabic, or explore Israeli and Palestinian culture, art, and food. Learn about other areas of the world that have similar conflicts.

Don't get discouraged at the seemingly endless nature of the conflict; anything worth solving is hard. If you're really committed to making a difference, ask a teacher or parent how you can do more. You can organize a school project or a community service program to help people in the Middle East. Remember that peace is something that starts on a personal level. Learning about a conflict like the fight over the Holy Land can teach you how to see things from many different perspectives and realize the importance of understanding. And remember, just because this fight has lasted for a century does not mean it has to continue for another.

Timeline

APPROXIMATELY 1900–1800 B.C.E. ▌ Religious scholars believe the prophet Abraham lived during this time period. Abraham leaves his home in Ur, which is now Iraq, to settle in Canaan, believed to be where modern Israel and the Occupied Territories are. Abraham's grandson Jacob and great-grandson Joseph move their family to Egypt.

APPROXIMATELY 1250 B.C.E. ▌ Religious scholars believe Moses leads the Israelites out of Egypt and into the Sinai desert. After 40 years, they cross the river Jordan into Canaan and during the next 200 years establish the Kingdom of Israel.

APPROXIMATELY 1000–920 B.C.E. ▌ King David captures Jerusalem. His son Solomon builds a temple there on what some scholars now believe is the Temple Mount. After Solomon's death, Israel splits into two Kingdoms—Israel and Judah.

722 B.C.E. ▌ Assyria conquers the northern Kingdom of Israel. The Israelites are exiled.

597 B.C.E. ▌ Babylon invades Judah. Many of the Jews are sent to cities near Babylon in modern-day Iraq. This begins the Diaspora. In exile, modern Judaism begins to evolve. A decade later Babylon captures Jerusalem and destroys the first Temple.

45 B.C.E. ▌ Rome conquers the Holy Land and eventually names it Palestina.

4 B.C.E. ▌ Birth of Jesus Christ.

66–70 ▌ Jewish political party called the Zealots leads a rebellion against Rome. Members manage to control parts of Palestina for four years, but the Romans retake Jerusalem and destroy the second Temple.

395 ▌ Roman Empire splits into two empires, Rome and Byzantium.

610 ▌ Muhammad receives his revelations, according to Islamic scholars. Beginning of Islam.

638 ▌ Arabian armies conquer Palestina, which they call Filastin, and Jerusalem. Al Aqsa mosque is soon built.

1096 ▌ Pope Urban II launches the first Crusade.

1099 ▌ Crusaders capture Jerusalem and slaughter all Jews and Muslims.

1187 ▌ Saladin retakes Jerusalem.

1306 ▌ France expels all its Jews.

1492 ▌ Shortly after completing the conquest of Spain, King Ferdinand and Queen Isabella order all Jews to either be baptized or be expelled. More than 150,000 Sephardic Jews leave for Ottoman Turkey, the Balkans, and North Africa. Thousands of others convert.

1516 ▌ Ottoman Turks take over Filastin.

1862 ▌ Moses Hess publishes "Rome and Jerusalem," one of the first Zionist books.

1882 ▌ Early Zionist communities are established in Filastin by Russian Jews fleeing pogroms. This marks the beginning of the first *aliya* (1882–1903).

1896 ▌ Austrian journalist Theodor Herzl publishes "The Jewish State," a pamphlet arguing for a Jewish state in the Holy Land or elsewhere.

1897 ▌ Herzl organizes the first Zionist Congress in Basel, Switzerland.

1904 ▌ The second *aliya* begins.

1914 ▌ World War I begins.

MAY 9, 1916 ▌ British and French leaders make the Sykes-Picot agreement, agreeing to carve up the Ottoman Empire into mandates after the war. Britain will get Palestine.

NOVEMBER 2, 1917 ▌ The British government issues the Balfour Declaration, endorsing a Jewish homeland in Palestine.

DECEMBER 9, 1917 ▌ British General Edmund Allenby's army enters Jerusalem. Soon all of Palestine is in British hands.

1919 ▌ Versailles Peace conference ends WW I and solidifies British and French control of the Middle East.

1919–23 ▌ The third *aliya*.

1920–21 ▌ Arabs riot against Jews in Hebron, Jerusalem, and Jaffa. Zionists organize militias for self-defense.

1924–1932 The fourth *aliya*.

1929 Arab riots start in Jerusalem, Hebron, and Safed.

1933 Adolf Hitler takes power in Germany.

1933–35 The fifth *aliya*.

1936–1939 The Palestinians revolt, attacking both British troops and Jewish settlers.

1937 The British Peel Commission responds to the revolt by recommending the partition of Palestine, with two-thirds for Arabs and one-third for Jews.

1939–1945 World War II and the Holocaust.

1946 The British government resists increased Jewish immigration from Europe to Palestine. Irgun responds with a terror campaign.

NOVEMBER 29, 1947 After the British give up, the United Nations steps in and votes to partition Palestine into two states. Jerusalem is to be internationalized. The Jews accept the plan, the Palestinians reject it. Fighting breaks out immediately.

APRIL 10, 1948 Irgun massacres Arab villagers at Deir Yassin. Palestinians begin fleeing villages. Palestinian forces retaliate three days later by attacking a medical convoy of wounded Zionists.

MAY 14, 1948 David Ben-Gurion declares Israeli independence in Tel Aviv.

MAY 15, 1948 Britain's mandate expires. War breaks out immediately as troops from Egypt, Jordan, Syria, Lebanon, and Iraq all invade. Egypt occupies the Gaza Strip; Jordan occupies the West Bank and East Jerusalem. The Israelis take the rest of the country, including West Jerusalem. Hundreds of thousands of Palestinians flee.

1949 Syria, Lebanon, and Egypt each make armistice agreements with Israel.

OCTOBER 29, 1956 In an alliance with Britain and France, Israel launches an attack on Egypt and soon takes the Sinai Peninsula. Under U.S. and Soviet pressure, Israel eventually withdraws.

MAY 1964 Arab heads of state led by Egyptian President Gamal Abdel Nasser establish the Palestine Liberation Organization in Cairo.

JUNE 5–10, 1967 ▓ The Six-Day War: After watching Syrian, Egyptian, and Jordanian troops prepare to attack, Israel strikes preemptively. The Israelis are victorious and occupy East Jerusalem, the West Bank, the Golan Heights, the Gaza Strip, and the Sinai.

FEBRUARY 3, 1969 ▓ Fatah leader Yasser Arafat wins the post of PLO executive committee chairman.

MARCH 8, 1969 ▓ Egypt begins a war of attrition against IDF troops in Sinai.

SEPTEMBER 1970 ▓ The PLO attempts to take over Jordan, where much of the population is Palestinian refugees. King Hussein puts it down and PLO guerrillas relocate to southern Syria and Lebanon.

SEPTEMBER 5–6, 1972 ▓ The Black September terrorist group takes Israeli Olympic athletes hostage in Munich. Terrorists kill two athletes, and nine other athletes die in an airport shoot-out.

OCTOBER 6–25, 1973 ▓ The Yom Kippur War: Egypt and Syria completely surprise Israel with an attack on Yom Kippur. Israel eventually pushes them back and retains its occupied territories, but the people are shaken.

NOVEMBER 19, 1977 ▓ Egyptian President Anwar Sadat goes to Jerusalem to offer peace in exchange for the Sinai. He recognizes Israel and addresses the Knesset.

SEPTEMBER 18, 1978 ▓ Sadat and Israeli Prime Minister Menachem Begin sign the Camp David peace accords. Israel withdraws from the Sinai, dismantling settlements in the process.

OCTOBER 6, 1981 ▓ Egyptian Islamists assassinate Sadat.

JUNE 6, 1982 ▓ Israel invades civil war–torn Lebanon to get at the PLO, reaching the outskirts of Beirut. Arafat and his group are forced to flee to Tunisia.

JUNE 6, 1985 ▓ Israel completes its withdrawal from most of Lebanon.

DECEMBER 9, 1987 ▓ The first intifada begins in Gaza.

DECEMBER 13, 1988 ▓ Arafat goes to the U.N., renounces terrorism, and recognizes Israel's right to exist. The next month, the U.S. government begins a dialogue with the PLO.

JUNE 1990 ▓ President George H. W. Bush severs ties with the PLO after Arafat refuses to condemn a terror raid by a radical PLO faction.

1991 In October, the United States and Soviet Union convene the Madrid Peace Conference, which brings Israel into direct negotiations with Jordan, Syria, Lebanon, and the Palestinians for the first time. Two months later the parties continue talks in Washington, D.C.

JANUARY 1993 Israeli-Arab talks in Washington prove futile, so Israel and the PLO begin secret talks in Oslo, Norway.

APRIL 16, 1993 The first suicide bombing by a Palestinian.

AUGUST 1993 The Israeli-PLO Declaration of Principles is announced to a startled world from Oslo. A month later, Arafat and Yitzhak Rabin shake hands on it at the White House.

FEBRUARY 25, 1994 Baruch Goldstein enters the Cave of Patriarchs during Muslim prayers and guns down 29 Palestinians before being killed.

MAY 1994 Israeli troops withdraw from Gaza and Jericho as the Palestinian Authority takes control.

OCTOBER 19, 1994 A Hamas suicide bomber blows up an Israeli bus in Tel Aviv, killing 22.

OCTOBER 26, 1994 Israeli and Jordanian leaders sign a peace treaty between their nations.

AUGUST 25, 1995 A woman blows up a bus in Jerusalem for Hamas. Five are killed.

SEPTEMBER 28, 1995 Interim agreements (Oslo II) give the Palestinian Authority control of more West Bank cities.

NOVEMBER 4, 1995 Rabin is murdered at a peace rally in Tel Aviv by Jewish student Yigal Amir.

FEBRUARY–MARCH 1996 A wave of suicide bombings across Israel kills 57 Israelis.

MAY 29, 1996 Likud Prime Minister Binyamin Netanyahu wins election. Soon he halts the Israeli withdrawal from the West Bank and restarts settlement construction.

MARCH 19, 1997 Netanyahu proposes final status talks at Camp David. Arafat rejects them.

MARCH 21, 1997 A suicide bomber attacks Tel Aviv, killing four.

AUGUST 12, 1997 Palestinians protest in Nablus, calling on Arafat to take a tougher line with the Israelis in peace talks.

OCTOBER 17–23, 1998 Netanyahu and Arafat, with the help of U.S. President Bill Clinton, negotiate the Wye River agreement. Israel will continue to transfer control of land and free Palestinian detainees. Arafat will crack down on terrorist factions and confiscate their weapons.

NOVEMBER 20, 1998 Israel transfers control of most remaining large population areas in the Occupied Territories to the Palestinian Authority.

DECEMBER 14, 1998 In front of Clinton, Arafat cancels the parts of the PLO charter that called for the extermination of Israel.

DECEMBER 20, 1998 Netanyahu stops implementing the Wye agreement, accusing Arafat of not carrying out his end.

MAY 17, 1999 Ehud Barak and the Labor Party defeat Netanyahu and Likud at the polls. Barak begins aggressive peace talks with both Arafat and Syria.

JULY 11–25, 2000 The Camp David peace talks between Barak and Arafat, intended to reach a final settlement between the Israelis and Palestinians, fail.

SEPTEMBER 28, 2000 Defense Minister Ariel Sharon visits the Temple Mount. The second intifada breaks out soon afterward.

SEPTEMBER 30, 2000 A 12-year-old Palestinian boy, Mohammed al Durrah is killed by crossfire during a shootout between militants and IDF forces. His death in his father's arms is caught on video and broadcast to the world.

OCTOBER 1–8, 2000 Arab Israelis protest their status and demonstrate their solidarity with Palestinians. Police kill 13.

OCTOBER 12, 2000 Two Israeli police get lost in the West Bank. Palestinian Authority police take them to a police station in Ramallah, where an angry mob gathers and eventually storms the station, beating the men to death on TV.

DECEMBER 17, 2000 Israel begins targeted killings of Palestinian leaders.

FEBRUARY 6, 2001 Sharon and Likud defeat Barak at the polls.

AUGUST 9, 2001 A suicide bomber hits a Jerusalem Sbarro restaurant, killing 15.

MARCH 27, 2002 A suicide bomber attacks a Passover seder in a Netanya hotel, killing 29.

MARCH 29, 2001 ▍ Operation Defense Shield—Israel reoccupies all of the West Bank except Jericho, arresting 8,500 Palestinians and besieging Arafat's compound in Ramallah.

APRIL 21, 2001 ▍ Israel withdraws from most of Ramallah but not Arafat's compound, demanding militants inside be turned over. The siege continues until May 20.

JUNE 2002 ▍ Sharon's government begins building a "security barrier" around portions of the West Bank. Some portions consist of wire and mesh fencing while other portions—cutting through populated areas like neighborhoods around Jerusalem—consist of 20-foot-high concrete walls.

JUNE 24, 2002 ▍ President George W. Bush calls for a Palestinian state, but says before that can happen, the Palestinians must elect new leaders and cease all terrorism. Israeli forces move back in to reoccupy most of the West Bank.

JULY 23, 2002 ▍ Israel drops a bomb on the home of a Hamas military leader, killing him and 12 others, including 9 children.

JANUARY 5, 2003 ▍ A double suicide bombing in Tel Aviv kills 23.

JANUARY 28, 2003 ▍ Sharon wins reelection by a wide margin.

APRIL 29, 2003 ▍ Under pressure to reform his government, Arafat allows the election of a Palestinian prime minister but retains tight control over the Authority.

NOVEMBER 24, 2003 ▍ Sharon announces his plan to unilaterally withdraw from the Gaza Strip and possibly from portions of the West Bank if the peace process continues to fail.

MARCH 22, 2004 ▍ Israeli planes drop a missile on Sheik Ahmed Yassin, the leader of Hamas, killing him instantly.

MAY 2004 ▍ Likud party members reject Sharon's proposal to unilaterally withdraw from Gaza. He pledges to rework the proposal and proceed. Extremist religious settlers begin to make veiled threats against Sharon's life.

JUNE 30, 2004 ▍ The Israeli Supreme Court rules that portions of the West Bank barrier violate the rights of Palestinians and orders 18 miles rerouted. But it rules the rest of the barrier legal.

JULY 2004 ▍ Fatah factions in Gaza—some loyal to Arafat and some frustrated with his leadership—begin to fight over who would control the Strip if Israel withdraws.

Acknowledgments

THE ISRAELI-PALESTINIAN conflict is a painful subject, and I often thought I would be happier if I just left it alone. But I'm not good at avoiding trouble. And many people—friends, colleagues, and complete strangers who read *Understanding September 11th*—encouraged me to write this. Thank you. I couldn't have done it without you.

I want to give special thanks to all the great people at Viking who made this possible, particularly Janet Pascal, Nancy Brennan, and Regina Hayes. I also want to thank my colleagues at *Time* who helped, especially Lisa Beyer, Susan Reed, and David Van Biema. And thank you to my fellow reporters in the John Edwards 2004 press corps, who assisted me while I tried to write in a van in the middle of Iowa.

There really should be two Franks on the front of this book. I am truly blessed to be married to my editor. Catherine, without you this would have been impossible. Thank you for your inspiration, energy, patience, wisdom, and willingness to work 24/7. Thanks for being my partner and best friend.

Glossary

ALIYA: Hebrew word meaning "ascent." It refers to the time when a Jew is called up to read the Torah in synagogue, and is also the term for a wave of Jewish immigration to the Holy Land.

ANTI-SEMITISM: Hostility toward Jewish people.

AL AQSA MARTYRS BRIGADES: A militant Palestinian group in Yasser Arafat's Fatah party. The group has used terrorist attacks—chiefly suicide bombings—against Israelis during the second intifada.

AL AQSA MOSQUE, AL MASJID AL AQSA: "The most distant mosque," named after a passage in the Qur'an. The mosque stands on top of the Temple Mount or Noble Sanctuary, and Muslims consider it the third most sacred mosque.

ARAB ISRAELIS: Muslims, Druze, and Christians of Palestinian origin who are citizens of Israel. They have the same rights as Jewish Israelis, but sometimes face discrimination.

ARAB LEAGUE: An organization of Arabic-speaking nations established in 1944, formally known as the League of Arab States.

BALFOUR DECLARATION: The 1917 government declaration named for British Foreign Secretary Lord Arthur Balfour, which promised that the British would create a Jewish homeland in Palestine.

B.C.E.: An abbreviation for "Before the Common Era," indicating a date before the year 1 in the modern Western calendar.

CAMP DAVID ACCORDS: The agreement signed by Israel and Egypt in 1978 at the U.S. presidential retreat in Camp David, Maryland, that created a framework for a peace treaty the following year.

CAVE OF PATRIARCHS: Also known as the Mosque of Abraham. Jews and Muslims both believe this shrine outside Hebron in the West Bank is the resting place of Abraham.

C.E.: An abbreviation for "Common Era," indicating a date from the year 1 or later in the modern Western calendar.

CHRISTIANITY: The world's largest religion, with two billion followers who believe the Jewish prophet Jesus Christ, who lived 2,000 years ago, was the Messiah and the son of God.

COLD WAR: Conflict between the United States and the Soviet Union that began shortly after World War II and ended in 1989. The two superpowers did not fight a real, or "hot," war, which would have been too dangerous, since after 1949 both had nuclear weapons. Instead they tried to gain influence in other countries throughout the world and spread their competing philosophies of democracy and communism.

COLONIALISM: The control and exploitation by one nation of a foreign territory or country for strategic and/or economic reasons.

CRUSADE: A military campaign fought in the name of Christianity or, more generally, for any religious cause.

DIASPORA: A Greek term meaning "a scattering of people," which refers to Jews living outside the Holy Land. It has recently been adopted by Palestinian refugees living outside the Holy Land.

DOME OF THE ROCK: A Muslim shrine atop the Noble Sanctuary, in Arabic Qubbat As Sakhrah. Muslims believe this is where Muhammad ascended to heaven.

DRUZE: A small religious community in the Middle East. Most Druze live in Israel, Syria, and Lebanon. Their faith began as an offshoot of Islam but has grown into a unique religion with elements of Judaism, Christianity, and Greek philosophy.

ERETZ YISRAEL: Hebrew for "Land of Israel," the area many Jews believe was controlled by the Kingdom of Israel in David and Solomon's time. Religious Zionists believe modern Israel should control all of that land, which includes the Occupied Territories.

FATAH: A political party and militant group founded by Yasser Arafat and colleagues in 1958. Originally dedicated to creating a Palestinian state in the entire Mandate by violent means, it is now a leading political party in the Palestinian Authority. It still controls several militant divisions that use terrorism.

FEDAY: Arabic for "one who sacrifices himself," a feday is a Palestinian guerrilla who raids Israel. The plural is fedayeen.

GAZA STRIP: A thin strip of land in the southwest corner of the old Palestine Mandate, running from Gaza City to the Egyptian border. The strip was controlled by Egypt from 1949 to 1967, after which it was occupied by Israel.

GOLAN HEIGHTS: A portion of Syria on the northeastern border of Israel. Israel occupied it during the Six-Day War and has held it ever since.

GULF WAR I: In August 1990, Iraq, governed by dictator Saddam Hussein, invaded its small neighbor Kuwait. In January 1991, the U.S. and a coalition of nations, including several Arab countries, sent their armies into Kuwait, liberating it.

GULF WAR II: Worried about the threat of Saddam Hussein to the rest of the Middle East and the possibility of his giving weapons of mass destruction to terrorists, the United States, led by President George W. Bush, invaded Iraq in 2003 with the help of Great Britain and other nations. American forces overthrew Hussein but faced continuing attacks by insurgents opposed to the occupation. U.S. forces have not found weapons of mass destruction.

GUSH EMUNIM: Hebrew for "bloc of the faithful," a religious organization that believes Israelis should settle as much of the Occupied Territories as possible to prevent the government from ever giving up the land.

HAGANAH: Jewish militia in Palestine during the Mandate period.

HAMAS: An acronym for Harakat al Muqawamah al Islamiyyah, Arabic for "Islamic Resistance Movement," a militant Palestinian organization of Islamists established in 1987 during the first intifada. Hamas members believe Palestinians need a country ruled by Islamic law, occupying all of the Holy Land.

AL HARAM AL SHARIF: Arabic for the Noble Sanctuary, the Muslim name for the hill in the center of Old Jerusalem; site of the Dome of the Rock and al Masjid al Aqsa, the Aqsa Mosque.

HEBREW: Ancient Jewish language used in the Jewish Bible. Zionists helped develop a modern version of the language, which is the official language of Israel.

HOLOCAUST: A term derived from the Greek for "sacrificing life by fire," Holocaust refers to the German Nazis' organized extermination of more than 11 million people, mostly Jews, but also Gypsies, communists, homosexuals, the physically and mentally disabled, and others. Jews sometimes call it the Shoah, Hebrew for "calamity."

HOLY LAND: The area in the Middle East that Jews, Christians, and Muslims believe is sacred, usually considered to encompass Israel and the Occupied Territories. Muslims also consider Mecca and Medina in Saudi Arabia holy land.

INTIFADA: Arabic for "shaking off," intifada refers to a violent uprising by Palestinians in the Occupied Territories against Israeli control. The first intifada raged intensely from 1987 to 1993. A second intifada began in the fall of 2000, after the peace process collapsed.

ISLAM: The religion of one billion people worldwide, Islam teaches that Allah is the one and only God and Muhammad was his final prophet. Islam's followers, Muslims, follow Muhammad's teachings.

ISLAMISM: A political belief that laws and government should be based on the teachings of Islam. Someone who believes in Islamism is an Islamist.

ISRAEL: A nation founded by Zionist Jews in 1948 in portions of the Palestine Mandate.

ISRAEL DEFENSE FORCES (IDF): Israel's army.

JUDAISM: A major worldwide religion of 13 million people, Judaism teaches that there is only one God, that his commandments must be obeyed, that all people are born good, and that God made a sacred agreement with the Jewish people four thousand years ago.

KINGDOM OF ISRAEL: The ancient kingdom the Jewish Israelites founded in the Holy Land around 1200 B.C.E. It later split into two kingdoms, Israel and Judea.

KINGDOM OF JERUSALEM: A country in the Holy Land founded by crusading knights from Europe in the twelfth century.

KNESSET: The Israeli legislature. The leader of the party with the largest number of seats is the prime minister, the head of the government.

MARTYR: A person who dies for his or her faith or for a cause. In Arabic, the word is *shaheed*.

MONOTHEISM: The belief in one god.

MOSSAD: The Israeli foreign intelligence organization. Observers consider it one of the world's most effective, rivaling America's CIA.

MUHAMMAD: Arab Prophet who Muslims believe founded Islam.

NATIONALISM: A philosophy that calls for uniting people by national identity.

OCCUPIED TERRITORIES: The West Bank and the Gaza Strip, which have been controlled by Israel since 1967, but are not part of Israel proper.

OSLO ACCORD: A framework for peace agreed to by the Israeli government and the Palestine Liberation Organization in 1993. Formally known as the Israeli-Palestine Liberation Organization Accord, the agreement created a peace process in which Israel began handing over portions of the Occupied Territories to Palestinians in return for recognition of Israel and an end to terrorist attacks.

PALESTINE: When the Romans conquered the Holy Land, they renamed it Palestina, which is Filastin in Arabic, and Palestine in English.

PALESTINE LIBERATION ORGANIZATION (PLO): An umbrella organization of several groups who share the common goal of creating a Palestinian nation. Yasser Arafat became chairman in 1969.

PALESTINE MANDATE: The colony in the Holy Land controlled by the British from 1917 to 1948.

PALESTINIAN AUTHORITY: The Palestinian government established by the Oslo Accord and given limited control over parts of the Occupied Territories. It consists of an executive branch made up of a president, a prime minister, twenty-four cabinet members, and a legislative branch.

PAN-ARABISM: An ideology that teaches that all Arab states should work together; it became popular during the 1950s and 1960s.

PROPAGANDA: One-sided information given to the public to try and sway opinions.

AL QAEDA: Islamist terrorist organization founded by Osama bin Laden of Saudi Arabia and other Arab veterans of the Afghan-Soviet War. The group is dedicated to attacking America and starting a war between the United States and the Muslim world. Al Qaeda hopes to unite Muslims into one Islamist nation. It has terrorist cells and affiliated extremists groups in dozens of countries.

AL QUDS: The Muslim name for Jerusalem, which means "the Holy City."

QUR'AN: The Muslim holy book, a collection of Allah's sermons recited by Muhammad. Sometimes spelled Koran.

RIGHT OF RETURN: The Palestinian demand that all Palestinians who fled the land that became Israel proper in the 1948 Israeli War of Independence should be allowed to return.

SHIN BET: The Israeli domestic intelligence service, responsible for security inside Israel and the Occupied Territories.

SINAI PENINSULA: A triangular piece of land in Egypt between the Suez Canal and the Israeli-Egyptian border. Israel occupied the Peninsula from 1967 to 1982.

SUICIDE BOMBING: An attack committed by someone who knows the explosion will take his or her own life as well as those of the people he or she is targeting.

TANACH: The Jewish bible, a Hebrew acronym formed from the names of three collections of sacred books: Torah, Neviim (Prophets), and Kesuvim (Writings).

TEMPLE MOUNT: The Jewish name for the hill in the center of Old Jerusalem. In ancient times, a platform and a Jewish temple were built on it.

TERRORISM: Violent acts against leaders or civilians in an attempt to create fear in people and force them to give in to political demands.

TORAH: The first five books of the Jewish bible.

TWO-STATE SOLUTION: The proposal to end the Israeli-Palestinian conflict by creating a Palestinian country, separate from Israel, in part or all of the Occupied Territories.

UNITED NATIONS: An international organization founded after World War II in the hope of solving international conflicts and problems.

WEST BANK: The area on the west bank of the Jordan River. It was part of the Palestine Mandate, then controlled by Jordan, then conquered by Israel in 1967. Some Jews refer to it as Judea and Samaria, names used during biblical times.

WESTERN WALL: A large side wall of the Temple Mount that Jews believe is the last remaining portion of the second Jewish Temple. Many Jews gather to pray there every day. It is sometimes called the Wailing Wall.

ZIONISM: Named for Zion, a Jewish word for the Holy Land, Zionism is the philosophy that Jews should have a nation of their own in the Holy Land.

Bibliography

Armstrong, Karen. *A History of God*. New York: Random House, 1993.

———. *Holy War: The Crusades and Their Impact on Today's World*. New York: Random House, 2001.

———. *Jerusalem: One City, Three Faiths*. New York: Random House, 1997.

Associated Press. "Israel's Wars—And How They Ended." April 5, 2002.

Bennet, James. "The Mideast Turmoil: How 2 Took the Path of Suicide Bombers." *The New York Times*. May 30, 2003.

Benvenisti, Meron. *Intimate Enemies: Jews and Arabs in a Shared Land*. Berkeley, Calif.: University of California Press, 1995.

Christison, Kathleen. *Perceptions of Palestine: Their Influence on U.S. Middle East Policy*. Berkeley, Calif.: University of California Press, 1999.

Cohn-Sherbok, Dan, and Dawoud El-Alami. *The Palestine-Israeli Conflict: A Beginner's Guide*. Oxford, England: Oneworld Publications, 2003.

Dawisha, Adeed. *Arab Nationalism in the Twentieth Century*. Princeton, N.J.: Princeton University Press, 2003.

Derfner, Larry. "Blow to Baruch Goldstein Cult." *Cleveland Jewish News*. November 26, 1999.

Friedman, Thomas L. *From Beirut to Jerusalem*. New York: Random House, 1995.

Haberman, Clyde. "Israelis Grieve, and Strike Back." *The New York Times*. August 11, 2001.

Halevi, Yossi Klein. "Kahane's Murderous Legacy." *The Jerusalem Post*. March 24, 1994.

BIBLIOGRAPHY

Hilberg, Raul. *The Destruction of the European Jews*. New Haven, Conn.: Yale University Press, 2003.

Hiro, Dilip. *The Essential Middle East*. New York: Carroll & Graf Publishers, 2003.

Holy Lands: One Place, Three Faiths. By the editors of *Life* magazine. Introduction by Thomas Cahill. New York: Time Inc., 2002.

Hourani, Albert. *A History of the Arab Peoples*. New York: Warner Books, 1991.

Kimmerling, Baruch, and Joel S. Migdal. *The Palestinian People: A History*. Cambridge, Mass.: Harvard University Press, 2003.

Lewis, Bernard. *The Middle East: A Brief History of the Last 2,000 Years*. New York: Scribner, 1995.

Lipstadt, Deborah. *Denying the Holocaust: The Growing Assault on Truth and Memory*. New York: Plume, 1994.

LoLordo, Ann. "For Palestinians, a Catastrophe." *The Baltimore Sun*. May 10, 1998.

McGeary, Johanna. "Inside Hamas." *Time*. April 5, 2004.

Neff, Donald. "Suez Crisis: How America Met Its First Test in Egypt." *U.S. News and World Report*. October 26, 1981.

Rees, Matt. "Hard Times, Hard Man." *Time*. November 27, 2000.

Said, Edward W. *The End of the Peace Process*. New York: Vintage Books, 2003.

Scherman, Rabbi Nosson, editor. *Tanach*. Brooklyn, N.Y.: Mesorah Publications, 2000.

Segev, Tom. *One Palestine, Complete*. New York: Henry Holt and Company, 2000.

Shipler, David K. *Arab and Jew: Wounded Spirits in a Promised Land*. New York: Penguin Books, 2002.

Simon, Jeffrey D. *The Terrorist Trap*. Bloomington, Ind.: Indiana University Press, 2001.

Struck, Doug. "Jewish Radicals Hostile to Arab-Israeli Harmony." *The Baltimore Sun*. November 6, 1994.

The World Factbook 2003. Washington, D.C.: Central Intelligence Agency, 2003.

Index

Numbers in italic indicate illustrations.